Suzie Edge trained as a molecular cell biologist before moving to clinical medicine, to spend more time talking to people, rather than just bugs in test tubes. She went on to work as a junior doctor in a variety of medical specialties including infectious diseases, haematology, and trauma and orthopaedic surgery. She recently completed an MLitt in Modern History to feed her fascination for the history of the human body and the history of medicine.

Always on the lookout for gory historical details, Suzie loves telling stories of how we have treated our human bodies in life and in death. She has over 325,000 followers on TikTok who love tuning into her stories of how famous monarchs met their end.

mortal monarchs

Dr SUZIE EDGE

WILDFIRE

First published in 2022 by
WILDFIRE
an imprint of HEADLINE PUBLISHING GROUP

First published in paperback in 2023 by
WILDFIRE
an imprint of HEADLINE PUBLISHING GROUP

5

Illustrations by Hayley Warnham

Cataloguing in Publication Data is available from the British Library

ISBN 978 1 4722 9423 4

Typeset in Adobe Garamond by CC Book Production

Printed and bound in Great Britain by
Clays Ltd, Elcograf S.p.A.

HEADLINE PUBLISHING GROUP
An Hachette UK Company
Carmelite House
50 Victoria Embankment
London EC4Y 0DZ

www.headline.co.uk
www.hachette.co.uk

For Howard, Liz, Derek, Kathryn and Charlotte

Contents

Introduction

In January 1066 Edward the Confessor, king of the English, stumbled. A clot was forming in the blood vessels within his brain. Soon the clot was dangerously lodged in a small artery. Behind it, the red blood cells and plasma carrying the oxygen, energy and nutrients backed up and pushed against the clot that would not budge. With Edward's blood unable to get through to his brain tissue, the cells starved of oxygen. Being demanding aerobes, his cells needed the blood supply to survive.

If enough of the brain was spared the ischaemia (lack of blood supply), then his body could survive, for now, but he would probably experience difficulties with moving limbs, speaking, or understanding. Edward had a series of strokes until eventually his brain shut down and he died. His body was embalmed and buried at Westminster where he had built the Abbey. In the first week of January, his ending sparked events that made 1066 one of England's most famous dates. The King was succeeded by his wife's brother, Harold Godwinson, but Harold did not see what was coming next. By Christmas of 1066, he too was dead, and another claimant was crowned king.

Despite the belief that monarchs were appointed by God, they were mere mortals like the rest of us. But despite being mere mortals, their deaths often meant so much. The death of a king could spell catastrophe for some or salvation for others, depending on who they had supported and who was to succeed. The new monarch could bring with them wars and bankruptcy, or they could bring peace and wealth. Whenever a monarch died there followed a time of uncertainty and concern. The stories of the monarchs' deaths tell us so much about their reigns and many of those tales were written to placate the newly crowned incumbent.

Edward the Confessor was a pious, gentle man, an intimation passed on to us by the religious chroniclers following his reign. We know Edward was a good man because history records a good ending for him. There was no need to create or tell us stories of a gruesome end for Edward, there were no stories of stinking putrefaction or ghastly death scenes as were bestowed on many unloved monarchs. His was a peaceful ending, a reflection of what we are meant to make of him. That's because the stories told about how monarchs died were never mere recordings of detail. Rather they are morality tales, meant for the people and posterity to remember their reign. Their deaths reflected their lives, and the quality of life under them. So the story of Edward's demise is a pleasant one. Those who followed Edward the Confessor to the throne were not always given the same treatment.

Clifford Brewer, the last surviving surgeon to have worked

during the D-Day landings in 1944, also shared our interest in the deaths of monarchs during his quieter moments. He studied the mortality of our kings and queens from William the Conqueror to Queen Victoria in his book *The Death of Kings*. His observations sometimes carried a surgical leaning, where a physician might make different interpretations.

As a medical doctor myself, who later also studied history, I became interested in the history of the human body and in the history of death. It fascinates me how these sometimes gruesome stories can be manipulated to defend or accuse, even after the body has taken its last breath. The lives of monarchs may have been very different to those of their people but I could see how the deaths of those monarchs reflected the deaths of everyone. This book aims to study the stories of the rulers' final days, updating our understanding of their deaths. Four more British monarchs have died and at least one has been found since Brewer's stories ended. It's time to re-evaluate how our monarchs died with a modern understanding of medicine and genetics, and in some cases shed new light on the stories of the kings and queens of England and Scotland.

It is my hope that as we understand more about the human body, we will also understand more about the monarchs who have shaped the near one thousand years since 1066. The more we know of the human body and medicine now, the more we can delve into the historical figures' insides, to understand what they may have gone through. These are, though, retrospective diagnoses and every argument is an interpretation based on current understandings. Academic historians might raise an eyebrow or

3

roll their eyes at anyone trying their hand at retrospective diagnosis. Attempting to diagnose a cause of death a few hundred years after the event is wrought with inconsistencies and difficulties in interpretation. However, the detailed records of monarchs' illnesses and final days make it much more possible to study their deaths. Through the changing fashions in the study of history and also in popular culture, the monarchs' lives have remained central to so much storytelling. The accounts of them are more accessible and widely known, far more than for most people in history. Most of all though, it is fun to mull over the potential pathologies and treatments given. With the best of the surgeons and physicians at hand, providing the very latest in care for ailing monarchs, we can see the medical beliefs, understandings and fashions of the day. We can see how they changed and not just in how the body was treated in life, but also in death. We see when autopsies became more common and how and why embalming practices changed. We can see, through the treatments given to the monarchs, how those treatments changed for everyone over a thousand years.

Each chapter brings a new monarch whose medical history we dive into. In retrospectively diagnosing any of our predecessors, monarchs or otherwise, we must be careful not to lay our own experiences of ill health onto theirs or stick strictly to modern ailments. Some diseases could well have come and gone in the last thousand years, diseases that we have no idea even existed.

How the kings and queens of England and Scotland have died has been a mix of the bizarre, accidental, painfully common and downright mysterious. There has been violence, infections, overindulgence and even the occasional regicide. There were plots, accusations, rivalries, and there was the ever-present menace of poison. Trauma was a constant threat, not just on the battlefield but also at play. Hunting and jousting were as dangerous as battle. More than one of the monarchs was injured or killed whilst at leisure. If our monarchs avoided a traumatic end then an infection was just as likely to strike them down. Dysentery, tuberculosis and smallpox played their part. There was rarely a death without a suspicion of murder. The whisper of poison was never far from the lips of those in power. Many monarchs who usurped their predecessor increased the risk of a similar lethal end for themselves. In short, if your hands were covered in blood when you took the crown, don't be surprised if a violent murder is coming your way too.

By the twentieth century the kings and queens had put aside axes through the head, pokers up the rear end and gushing dysentery for more of the chronic lifestyle-related diseases of the lungs and heart that claim most of our lives today. When it came to the monarchs though, the last century was not without its own controversy.

Some members of the royal family are largely forgotten while others are seen as icons in academia and in popular culture. So much was recorded of their demise, and of the accompanying ceremony, that studying their deaths also becomes a history of how we've treated, cared for and disposed of bodies throughout time. Of course for everyone else it was most likely a mass grave during a plague or suffering as the whole village was ravaged by pestilence, famine or war. The bodies of the kings and queens were no different to others, and so were subject to the same decay and indignity of death.

However, in the case of monarchs, we can be assured that the stories told and the histories that we have were embellished to suit the needs of those writing them. The agendas of the writers, the religious chroniclers, always learned men, set the tone and dictated our understanding. It was they who could bestow saintly wholesomeness on someone they felt should be admired, or devilish putrefaction on someone they wanted to paint in a bad light. At the stroke of an inky quill they would do just that, and their stories are still told today.

Remains of the kings and queens, whilst often given lavish over-the-top send-offs by those left behind, were not always allowed to simply rest in peace. The sacking of graves looking for lead and riches, the pulling down of abbeys and simple curiosity has led to many tombs being opened, prodded, poked and stolen from. For Richard III, the discovery of his remains makes for a wonderful tale of persistence, problem-solving and luck.

It is time to pull on the rubber gloves and take a deep dive into the blood and guts of a thousand years of royal deaths.

Suzie Edge
March 2022

Harold Godwinson

Died 1066

Harold looks up at the wrong moment.

From the classrooms of the Ragged Schools to the halls of Eton College, it has been the duty of every English schoolchild to learn that at the Battle of Hastings in 1066, King Harold was killed by an arrow that hit him in the eye.

As a nearby soldier shouted, 'Watch out,' Harold turned to look up at the sky above the battlefield at the worst possible moment. The cold sharp metal struck his face and burst open his eyeball. The juices from his eye lubricated the arrow as it tore through his retina, broke through the bone of his skull and lodged in the frontal lobe of his brain. This story will come up again and again, at the pub quiz at your local on Friday night, and in conversation with Granny over Trivial Pursuit at Christmas: in 1066 the English King Harold II took an arrow in the eye at Hastings, thus starting the Norman Conquest and the reign of William the Conqueror.

It is the fate of those same schoolchildren to learn, at some shatteringly disappointing moment later in life, that the details of Harold's demise are likely nonsense, and that this is probably not how Harold Godwinson was killed. Sincerest of apologies if this is such a moment.

Though it might still be taught in our schools, there is a strong argument against Harold's death being arrow induced. But the modern theory that the arrow narrative is a pack of lies is not going to stop us contemplating the notion of taking one in the eye on an eleventh-century battlefield.

The enduring image of an embroidered Harold, clutching at an arrow lodged in his face, comes from a most wonderful piece of art that has survived the centuries, the Bayeux Tapestry. The incredibly well-preserved, 70-metre-long embroidered work tells us one version of the story of the Norman invasion. Whose version it is is not entirely clear and nor is it clear exactly what happened to Harold. The iconic image of the soldier grasping at the arrow in his face comes below the text *Hic Harold Rex Interfectus Est* (Here King Harold has been killed).

Those with a keen eye on the Bayeux Tapestry will notice the depiction of another man, also under that text. This man has fallen, and he is being run through by a sword-wielding horseman. This other man might have been Harold all along. If, however, we might read the Bayeux Tapestry in sequence, then Harold was struck in the eye with an arrow, fell to the ground (changing his socks on the way) and was then killed, chopped to pieces by swordsmen. It is intriguing that in a copy of the

Bayeux Tapestry from the 1700s there is no arrow in the face of the gentleman in question. Could it have been added later? During a restoration perhaps?

Being hit in the face with an arrow was not necessarily an immediate death sentence. At least two other monarchs can testify to that. Henry V of England (whilst he was Prince of Wales) and Philip II of Macedon (father of Alexander the Great) both had battle arrows pulled from their skulls and survived. Sadly, James IV of Scotland cannot join the club: an arrow in the face killed him at Flodden in 1513.

That is not to say that King Harold definitely didn't die from an arrow in the eye, bearing in mind that he certainly met his demise on the day of the battle in October of 1066. We do know his life did not end in a long, drawn-out agonising scene on a deathbed. It was not caused by sepsis with a grim wound-site infection spreading across his face. He did not lie in pain for weeks, with his wounds tended by an already grieving widow whilst his brain shut down. Something killed Harold on the day. It was instant and if it were an arrow, it would have travelled far through his eye and through the skull behind it, to do damage deep inside the brain. It would have caused a bleeding and a swelling in the brain, meaning that oxygenated blood could no longer get through and sustain brain function.

Aerodynamic, fast and sharp, a metal arrowhead fixed to a wooden arrow, shot from a Norman bow, could easily cut through the tissue of the face, the eyeball, the thin bone of the sockets and the jelly-like brain tissue that sits behind them. The eyeball itself is extremely vulnerable, sitting outside the protective bony skull. It is merely a squidgy ball of fluid, held and controlled by the small muscles around it.

If a Norman had punched Harold in the face or had used a blunt weapon, the eyeball would have been pushed backwards into the socket rather than being permitted to explode. The pressure of that force can be great enough to cause a break in the thin bony layer of the eye socket behind it. The thin layer of bone is there to take one for the team, releasing the energy and stopping the eyeball from impending messy explosion. It is a bit like how a modern car will crumple around a passenger in a high impact car crash. Such a traumatic event does not ever look survivable, but it is the crumpling of the car that saved the occupant by absorbing the energy of the crash.

The fracture of the socket, as an indirect blow to the thin bone caused by pressure through the eye, is known as a blowout fracture. So, blowout fractures defend the eye against blunt forces, but sharp, fast arrows are a different matter. Once through the eyeball and the socket wall, the arrow would encounter soft brain tissue, having avoided the hard skull that protects the rest of the head.

At the front of the brain, where the arrow tip would strike once it got through the sockets, is the frontal lobe. The frontal lobe is so named, not surprisingly, because it is at the front. Though it was named logically, the frontal lobe deals instead with emotion. We might surmise that if Harold took a sharp blow to the frontal lobe, it may well have momentarily rendered him emotionally disinhibited, and he might have been a little bit sweary. Frontal lobe injuries do manifest in sufferers acting out of character if they are not immediately fatal.

If we are looking for an injury that killed Harold instantly, the arrow would have to have sliced through the brain and its blood vessels. This would have set off a cascade of bleeding and swelling, and pushed the brain matter against itself and the skull, until blood could no longer move about and provide oxygen to the brain tissues. With a traumatic brain injury of this nature, it would not be long until unconsciousness and death.

Harold may not have been killed instantly by the arrow in his eye, but he could well have been inconvenienced enough to be caught and hacked apart by swordsmen. Guy, Bishop of Amiens, in his 'Song of the Battle of Hastings', the earliest contemporary source of the events, said that Harold was dismembered by four knights, including William of Normandy. They would claim Harold's death was at the hand of the all-conquering William, of course. There are many versions, some portray facial arrows, some do not.

It will become a theme when recounting the deaths of kings and queens that these stories are always varied and contrary. They are often commenting on the political, religious or moral nature of the monarch and trying to legitimise the reign of whoever came next. Propaganda, confusion and contradictory accounts are what can make the manner of a sovereign's death even gorier, and with that even more meaningful. Often the stories told of what happened to the monarchs give us insight into the political context, particularly of the monarch who came next.

Harold was dead, by arrow or by sword, and his body was held by the conquering Normans. Harold's widow Edith was brought over to the Norman camp to identify the body thought to be her husband. The face was mutilated so she could perhaps only provide an answer by recognising other distinguishing marks, in places familiar only to her.

Harold's mother went to William (whom we can now call The Conqueror) and asked him for her son's body back, offering a gold reward. William refused her, worried that the body would be used as relics, or as a shrine to martyrdom. As William himself had dug up the body of St Valery for moral support before he crossed the Channel, he was not wrong that this might be the fate of Harold's remains. Also, maybe onlookers would notice he did not have an arrow protruding from his face and that would ruin a thousand years of a good story.

The whereabouts of Harold Godwinson's final resting place is still up for debate, and some are looking to exhume what they think are his bones in the search for an answer.

When in 1954 workmen were lifting an old rotten floor at Holy Trinity Church in Bosham, Sussex, an Anglo-Saxon coffin was found. Bosham was Harold's birthplace and local historians believed that these could be the remains of Harold. With the head and part of one leg missing, this pattern of injury was consistent with Guy d'Amien's song describing Harold's last moments. The Diocese of Chichester refused an exhumation request in 2003, ruling that the chances of true identification were not high. Exhumation for sentiment or to satisfy curiosity on so little evidence was thought sensational, particularly as the task was to be paid for by a television company. It was likely to be a futile project anyway. If anything did remain of the bones found in 1954, the chance of anyone being able to extract DNA would be small and parts of the bones would need to be destroyed in the process. Even if DNA could be extracted, there would need to be a comparator, a living person who could for sure be a descendant of Harold Godwinson himself, nearly 1,000 years on. Carbon dating is not accurate enough to be conclusive that these remains belong to Harold, and are not from a generation above or below the King.

To dig up the grave of a Christian burial, whether it be Harold or not, would be standing teetering at the top of a slippery slope, and set a dangerous precedent. A floodgate would be opened that would allow for the exhumation of, well, everyone mentioned in this book for a start, and then who?

Most academics believe that the evidence points to Harold having been interred at Waltham Abbey. Some accounts state that the King was buried at sea, others say his resting place is somewhere near the coast, deliberately unmarked so that he would not be turned into a relic by rebels fighting the Normans. At the spot where Harold is supposed to have lost his life stands Battle Abbey, or what remains of it, but what remains of Harold's remains, remains a mystery.

Whether or not Harold took an arrow in the eye that day is a question unlikely ever to be answered. If he did, it may not have ended his life instantly, it may have just rendered him powerless against the mob surrounding him with swords and spears. The arrow in the eye story most likely represents a statement against the King: that he was not actually the true king. William's claim was tentative at best but the Normans felt that Harold broke the oath that he had made to William of Normandy, and he got his just deserts. His perjury was paid for by the symbolic punishment of the day for traitors, that of blinding. Harold was to be depicted for the next 1,000 years as the blinded king who had betrayed his oath. It will not be the last time we encounter a death story that conveys the writer's agenda around the memory of the deceased, rather than a true articulation of the moment of their departure.

William I

Died 1087

Duke William of Normandy was the bastard who was victorious at the Battle of Hastings in 1066. He really was called William the Bastard. We are not just calling him names for invading England. He was the illegitimate son of Robert the Magnificent and Heleva of Falaise, but we shall call him Duke William of Normandy for now, as it's better for the children. William survived the fight and so the Norman duke was able to claim the throne of England.

William believed the throne of England was rightfully his, promised to him by his distant cousin Edward the Confessor. He felt it was an arrangement that the new king Harold had sworn to uphold, and so an angry William went looking for what he thought was his. Now known as William the Conqueror, his reign began on Christmas Day in that infamous year of 1066.

William's post-coronation shenanigans included building new castles, settling his Norman nobles in England and the Harrying of the North. He placed his own clergymen in powerful church positions, pushing out the locals. He ordered the compilation of the Domesday Book, which was a record of the people and their land, or rather, William's new land. He did not bother to hang around too long in England though; back he went to France where the weather was somewhat preferable. It is hard to fault him for that.

In the summer of 1087, twenty-one years after the Battle of Hastings, William of Normandy was still out there fighting and pillaging. As he rode his horse through the streets of Mantes after a raid, he might well have been brooding over the French monarch's words. King Philip had pointed out that he looked fat like a pregnant woman. William had put on weight during his years as king of England. Around him the city was burning as his pillaging troops set alight the houses, causing chaos. A burning building sent up a lively hot spark and William's horse was spooked. Dobbin reared up and came down with a crash. William's giant frame, which had grown much too large in celebration of all the conquering, was thrown forward, his ample belly hitting the heavy iron pommel of his saddle.

The pressure on his abdomen, which pushed his insides back against the hard bones of his spine and pelvis, was enough to squeeze and split one of his organs open. A perforated bowel is the most quoted cause of death for William but it could have been either bowel or bladder, or perhaps even his urethra. In an injury such as a bowel perforation, a doctor would expect to hear of a painful distention of his abdomen, accompanied by vomiting; there was mention of his moaning in pain, but bloating and vomiting were not noted in reports of the King's death. Perforation of his bowel would have meant that the bowel's contents – the celebratory burgers and beers from so much conquering – which are usually separated from the peritoneum (the lining of the abdominal wall) by the walls of the bowel, would spill out, leaving faeces and bacteria free to cause trouble. The result is peritonitis – inflammation, and infection of the peritoneum. Untreated, peritonitis can lead to a painful death. Nowadays such a case would require a surgeon, an anaesthetist, an army of theatre nurses, intensive care nurses and a holy grail full of antibiotics. Orderic Vitalis, the chronicling monk, made no mention of an ICU admission but we must remember his account was written a few years after William's death, so he may have missed a detail or two.

Alternatively, the forceful crash of William's lower abdomen against the saddle's pommel could have perforated the rider's bladder or even his urethra (the tube that brings urine from the bladder down to the outside world). It is an injury that, though rare, could occur with an eye-watering, forceful shove of a saddle between the legs.

A perforation of the bladder would have been signalled by haematuria (blood in the urine), which again one would expect to have seen commented on in the accounts. Leakage of urine out of a split in the bladder wall can result in infected collections where you do not want them to be, and then in potentially deadly sepsis. If urine can't get out of the urethra, then it backs up to the kidneys, which can affect their function. If for any reason kidneys cannot filter blood, there is life-threatening trouble ahead.

Whatever was perforated, be it bowel, bladder, or urethra,

the injury brought about William's death. It took a few weeks though, and William had asked to be taken to the Priory of St Gervais at Rouen, Normandy's capital, where his bishops could tend to him. The chronicler Orderic wrote that in the time he had remaining, William was at least repentant, sorry for all the brutality, especially in England. He also had time to make plans for his sons and his lands, making William Rufus king of England and Robert Curthose Duke of Normandy. William I, King of the English and Duke of the Normans, died of complications stemming from an internal rupture of an organ on 9 September 1087. He was lucid in the morning and then he was dead. He was fifty-nine years old.

The story of what happened to William the Conqueror did not end there. Of course not. As soon as the King was dead, pillaging broke out and the nobles around him went off to protect their own lands and belongings. They left behind servants who pilfered all the King's belongings for themselves, even his finery and clothes, leaving his body unceremoniously dumped on the floor of his bedchamber. It is a story often repeated to demonstrate the consequences of being an unliked king. William was considered deceitful and ill-educated, culturally inadequate and unworthy, and his death story became an extension of that unworthiness.

Very soon the King's cold, dead body started to discolour. It was recovered from the bedchamber floor but there was little dignity in what was to come. His courtiers took a long time to decide how to honour him, how and where to bury him and who to invite to the after-party. It took for ever. The Archbishop of Rouen eventually declared that the body of the King should be taken to the monastery of St Stephen in Caen – but who was around to deal with it, embalm it or remove the smelly parts? There was one obstacle after another. On the way to Caen the procession had to stop to contend with a fire that broke out. All bodies begin to smell, even a king's. A knight called Ascelin of Caen came forward to claim that the church where William was to be buried had been built on land belonging to his father, land that had been stolen by William of Normandy. He wouldn't let the burial take place until they paid him off, only then did he agree they could go ahead. Can't think what made him change his mind.

All the while William's rotting corpse was swelling, getting bigger and bigger. Bodies swell after death because the mechanisms in place to keep the bowel contents inside the bowel fail and so all the foul contents leak out. The bacteria are freed and can go to lunch, burping and farting as they munch away on yummy dead-king stew. The gases swell the body and if you try, as they did, to shove that swollen, gas-filled corpse into a stone coffin, something is going to give way and explode, and it won't be the coffin. It's hard to imagine quite how bad the exploded king corpse must have smelled when the rotting remains burst free. The senser burners swung from side to side on their chains ahead of the procession, spreading their smoke of frankincense and spices, but they had no effect. The putrefaction in the air hit the nostrils hard. They had to finish the ceremony and get out fast.

Anyone associated with William might well have been accustomed to corpses lying about. Before the Battle of Hastings,

William waited for the weather to turn so that he could sail his army across the Channel, he needed a way to keep the mercenary troops on side while they waited. They were at the town of St Valery so it seemed a perfectly normal thing to do to dig up the body of the town's namesake and parade it in front of the troops, asking them all to pray for victory over his remains. Unlike William, though, St Valery was not the explosive type. He was a saint, so there were no stories of him exploding like the rotten king.

Putrefaction is a trope to brand the memories of the kings thought unworthy. William was remembered as a tyrant who disrespected England and so it is no surprise to hear of his stuff being looted and of this bodily decay. If an intact, untouched body was a sign of saintliness, a stinking and putrefied body, exploding and seeping rotting juices, surely demonstrated the opposite.

William Rufus, the son who was to become the next king of England, commissioned a tomb for his late father, and under it the first William did surprisingly well to rest in peace for 500 years. The Pope let someone open his tomb to have a look in 1522, when all was found to be well. He was reinterred, but forty years later a Calvinist mob broke in. They were expecting to find riches, and when they found nothing of use, they sacked the grave. What was left was again reinterred, but was later destroyed during the French Revolution. The plunderers were looking for lead to make musket balls. One single thigh bone, a left femur, was rescued and reburied. In the 1960s the single femur was found again. A thigh bone, the largest bone in the body, can tell us quite a lot, even a lonely single one. They give clues about the height and health of their owner. This one came from a man measuring between 5 feet 9 and 5 feet 11. It was thought to be all that remains of William I and it was buried again in 1987, to mark 900 years since William the Conqueror's death. On his tomb, a Latin inscription in marble slab tells us:

Here lies the invincible William the Conqueror,
Duke of Normandy and King of England,
founder of the house,
who died in the year 1087.

Can we define invincible? Well, I suppose his thigh bone has been, so far.

William II

Died 1100

Not to be outdone by his father's nicknames (William the Conqueror, William the Bastard), William II was known as William Rufus, meaning William the Red, because of his red complexion. Rufus was not the first-born son of William the Conqueror, he was the third. They lost their brother Richard in a hunting accident in the New Forest when Rufus was a teenager. Remember that important nugget, it reappears later. Clearly the New Forest is a dangerous place for princes – or Richard's death there gave someone an idea thirty years later.

Rufus had another older brother, Robert. He was a bit wayward and sided with the Conqueror's enemy, the king of France. Though he made up with his father towards the end, Robert had not earned the throne of England. Instead, he was given the duchy of Normandy without England. England was given to Rufus. Their youngest brother, Henry, was not given land, but got £5,000 upon his father's death. He was the sort of lad that had it weighed and measured on receipt, just to make sure he had been given the exact promised amount. When their father was buried, eventually, the sibling rivalries intensified, but Henry had the last laugh.

As kings go, William Rufus did a reasonable job. He defended his father's kingdom and kept rebellions at bay. He was a respected military general and had a reputation for courage and good luck. He was known to be generous to his loyal soldiers, who were keen to obey their king as there was a high price for disloyalty and punishments were severe and brutal.

However there were many who were not happy with the King, and the Church was chief among them. William had achieved his military might and added to his personal riches at the expense of the Church and rebel barons. He was slow to appoint clergy so he could use the lands and riches for himself. His attitude was distinctly anti-clerical and contemptuous of religion. His court was flamboyant and hedonistic, and the monastic chroniclers did not hold back in their equally contemptuous descriptions of William Rufus. The chroniclers, who happened to be religious men and held in contempt by Rufus, wrote of him as a waster, a womaniser and, worst of all, ungodly and deserving of what was to come his way.

What came his way happened on a fine day in early August in the year 1100. William had woken early, having had rather a lot to drink the night before. He was startled from a dream where he had had a conversation with the devil, who told him that he would be seeing him tomorrow. He was also told by the monks that they had had visions of terrible things ahead. William was not impressed or bothered, so they went hunting that afternoon.

William II

As they made ready, he handed two of his arrows to his companion, Walter Tyrell, Lord of Poix. *'Bon archer, bonnes flèches,'* he said – 'Good arrows for the good archer'. One might wonder if the arrows actually had William's name on them.

William's brother Henry was in another hunting party elsewhere in the forest. The game was afoot. A stag went by, Walter Tyrell took aim, and his arrow glanced off a tree and hit the King in the chest. This was not good. An arrow piercing the chest, with its sharp pointed iron head slicing between ribs, would hit either lung tissue or major vessels, or even the heart. Hitting a lung would mean the lung tissue being opened to the outside world, and air and blood could get drawn into the cavity between the pleura (the lining of the lungs) and the lung tissue. This haemo-pneumothorax not only means a lung that's not functioning, exchanging the gases that are required for the living cells, but the pressure can push against the heart. Once pierced, a major blood vessel such as the aorta, the artery that takes the blood from the heart to the rest of the body, will pour the blood out into the surrounding tissue instead. Each new beat of the heart deposits more blood where it should not be. With less and less blood to pump, the body recognises a reducing blood pressure and the heart starts to pump harder and faster. Catecholamines (the stress hormones) will be released that will tighten blood vessels, increasing the action of the heart, which will try its best to compensate. Rufus would have been gasping for air as his body struggled to provide more oxygenated blood to the tissues which by now are wondering where the blood has gone, especially the brain. If the tear in the vessel where blood is pouring out is not fixed, the compensation mechanisms will be working in vain.

If this huge pool of blood in the surrounding tissues grows, it will push onto the heart itself, the build-up of pressure will tamponade (compress the heart), fixing it, giving it no room to fill with blood and pump it out. If the sharp metal arrowhead tore through the heart itself, the damaged heart muscle would instantly struggle to coordinate the squeeze and to pump the blood. In either of these situations, the result will be a heart that can't pump or has nothing to pump.

While his body tried to compensate, to keep him alive despite overwhelming loss of blood, William broke the shaft of the arrow that hit him. He fell, pushing what was left further into his chest, and he breathed his last. To survive such an injury, you would need almost instant emergency pre-hospital surgery to stop the bleeding. Fibrillation of the heart muscle occurs as it can no longer beat effectively, and the heart muscle movement becomes erratic. For William Rufus, this scenario needs far more medical attention than a twelfth-century companion of the King could provide. Besides, they had all run off anyway. They did not want to be caught with, and blamed for, a dead king. The story told, of a king's body being left for dead by his companions, represented a time of fear once again. Tyrell fled, first to France and then onward to crusade. He did not attend the funeral of the dead king. Not many did, not even the King's brother, Henry.

Nobody was left to deal with the King's newly deceased corpse. It's a familiar story and one we heard with his father, William the Conqueror, thirteen years before. A dead king meant a time of change and potential lawlessness until he was replaced. Some servants were left to manhandle the King's dead body. Blue blood dripping onto their clothes and hands, they hauled him into a cart. The last of his air gurgled up through frothing blood in his throat as he was conveyed in the cart to Winchester.

William Rufus had no children. His heir would have to be one of his brothers, Robert or Henry, and as Robert was not in England, here was Henry's chance. Henry, having heard about his brother's death, rode straight away, not to his brother's side, but to Winchester.

There was more than one account of the events of that day. Another writer, in France, the Abbot Sergerius of St Denis stated that his good friend Tyrell was not even there in the forest that day. Tyrell didn't confess on his deathbed either, which was usually the time to bare all, so maybe he did not do that dastardly deed that our history books have laid upon him. Those who believe the King was assassinated argue that Tyrell was a good shot. He was not incompetent and therefore was unlikely to accidentally shoot the King.

A few days later, on Sunday, 5 August 1100, rather than turn up to mourn at his brother's funeral in Winchester, Henry was in London, being crowned Henry I, King of England, by Bishop Maurice. He wanted to be inaugurated quickly before the return of his older brother Robert Curthose, from his crusade. In this time when no king meant no law, everyone was happy to see a new king crowned so speedily.

Before these unfortunate events in the woods, the Pope had been considering excommunicating Rufus from the Church because of his contemptuous and irreligious behaviour. Henry, however, was supported by the Church. The accounts of the death of William II, written during the reign of Henry by monastic chroniclers, were not going to start throwing around accusations of assassination, but we can. Henry had the motive, he had little regard for Rufus's body after his demise, and interestingly, he had seen the deaths of both his older brother Richard, and his nephew (also Richard, son of Robert Curthose) occur as the result of arrow accidents while hunting in the forest. When he heard of his brother's death he did not hang about. He rushed straight off to Winchester to the crown treasury, and he was crowned only three days later. None of that sounds like the work of an innocent brother.

The remains of William Rufus have been hard to pin down, if not quite as hard as Rufus himself. He was buried at Winchester Cathedral but was later lost. For hundreds of years, it has been thought that the bones of William Rufus were held with the bones of other Anglo-Saxon rulers and a couple of bishops, within six mortuary chests held at Winchester. The bones were gathered when the original tombs were ransacked and now there is a list of twelve possible owners, but nobody knows exactly who the bones belonged to. Recent DNA analysis has shown twenty-two different people, only one of whom could be identified – Queen Emma of Normandy. William Rufus did not rest in peace, but at least he is not alone in the coffin chests, as he was on the day he was abandoned by his companions.

A stone in the New Forest marks the spot where our story of today played out, 900 years ago. Whether it's on the site of a dreadful royal accident or a monstrous murder, we'll never know. It is hard to imagine William's brother Henry I visiting to pay his respects.

Henry I

Died 1135

> *'A king is like a fire*
> *If you are too close, you burn*
> *If you are too far away, you freeze.'*
> Petrus Alfonssi, doctor to Henry I of England

Henry I, son of William the Conqueror and younger brother of William Rufus, also had a nickname, but not one we hear used as often. He was known as Henry Beauclerc, a French name meaning 'good clerk', because he was literate and educated. A well-read chap, one might say. He was more of a diplomat than a fighter like his brother William Rufus, and perhaps this counts against the accusation he assassinated his big brother in the New Forest in 1100. During Henry's reign, the death of William Rufus was firmly put down to an accidental arrow in the chest. Without a monarch breathing down our necks, we can say without fear of execution that Henry was very possibly behind his brother's death, wanting to take the throne of England. Of course, it is easy to accuse someone of murder when they have been dead for 900 years.

After his brother's demise and Henry's very quick departure for Winchester, he was coronated in London only a couple of days later. Henry I was thirty-two years old when he took the crown as king of England, and he ruled for the next thirty-five years. To talk about the death of Henry I, one needs the context of his life, especially as we've seen a monarch's death is often used as a commentary, or even an attack, on their reigns, even long after they have gone.

The monastic chroniclers felt that Henry's court was far more wholesome than his big brother's licentious court had been. They much preferred him however he might have acquired the throne. Even children remember the phrase 'A surfeit of Lampreys' that became associated with Henry I's demise, even if they remember nothing else about him. Hold on to your slippery lampreys, we will get to them a bit later.

Born in Selby in about 1068, Henry Beauclerc, that well-known Yorkshireman, grew up to do his very best for the population of England. Henry had relations with any woman who happened to pass by. He had at least twenty-four children, only two of whom were legitimate though. His son and heir, William, and his daughter Matilda, were both born of his marriage to Matilda of Scotland (also known as Edith – obviously). Marrying Matilda of Scotland meant that he was married to the daughter of the Scottish king, Malcolm III – his nickname 'Canmore' literally means 'big head' – and Margaret of Wessex. Margaret was known as the Pearl of Scotland, later Saint Margaret, but she was also sister to Edgar the Atheling, the last male member of the House of Wessex. This was an excellent political match.

Away from his marriage, nine of Henry's illegitimate children were married off to various royal houses of Europe when he became king. He used them as offerings in his diplomatic dealings. Sadly, Henry's children did not all end up with happy endings. The *White Ship* disaster played a huge role in what was to become of the line of succession after Henry's death.

It was a freezing cold but calm night in November 1120. Henry, his family and 250 of his nobles were due to travel back across the Channel from France to England. A man called Henry Fitzstephen stepped forward. His father's ship, years before, had been used to convey William of Normandy, Henry's father, across the Channel, and Fitzstephen asked that he might do the same for the Conqueror's son. Henry had already made plans and did not wish to deviate from them, but sure, his son William, the heir, and the others could travel across on *The White Ship* if they so wished. The travellers were in the mood for a party and the wine started to flow. Soon passengers and crew alike were heavily under the influence, singing songs and dancing, making merry. Orders were given that the ship be sailed as fast as possible, to try to race the ship that Henry I had set sail in hours before. Just out of harbour, the ship struck a rock and capsized. On that calm but very cold night, with winter on the horizon, all but one of the souls that had been aboard *The White Ship* died in the icy waters.

When thrown into icy waters, even in calm seas, the physiological responses of the body can be rapidly lethal. The first reaction is cold -water shock, which causes a sudden loss of control over breathing. The automatic response is to take one or more huge gasps followed by hyperventilation, an increase in the rate of breathing. The gasp may well mean that water is inhaled into the lungs, which would impinge gas exchange. With the sudden reduction in oxygen getting to the blood, the body increases the breathing rate further. This is all uncontrollable. The blood vessels contract, and up go the blood pressure and the heart rate. More than that, the cold water around the ears can bring on vertigo and disorientation, worsened in this scenario by the passengers of *The White Ship* being drunk on wine. In these dark waters they might have struggled to know which way was up. Some of the passengers aboard *The White Ship* likely succumbed to cold -water shock immediately. If the passengers and crew survived the initial plunge, then without rescue they would have succumbed to hypothermia. Hundreds died in this way when *The White Ship* hit the rock.

The lone survivor, who was said to have been wrapped in a sheepskin coat, clung to a rock and survived the night. He was a butcher from Rouen, named Berold. He was not part of the noble's party, but had followed them to try to recoup the money that he said he was owed by members of the travelling party. He was the only one left to tell the tale, and it was a fantastic one at that: he claimed to have seen the heir to the throne moved onto a small vessel, where he might have been safe from the crash. The young heir heard his sister's cries in the water and went back to find her, only for the smaller boat to be surrounded by those in the water who, when they all tried to clamber aboard to safety, capsized that too, dragging them all under. Cries were heard from the shore but were attributed to the noisy revellers having an alcohol-fuelled night of fun aboard the boat.

When all was over, nobody could bring themselves to tell Henry the news. A young boy was pushed forward to tell the King that he had lost at least four of his children that night, and so many of his family's closest nobles. Henry's succession was in question.

Henry I holds the monarchs' record for having the most children and still his death sparked a succession problem. His male heir had gone down with *The White Ship*. After Good Queen Matilda died in 1118, Henry married again but sired no more legitimate children. Despite having his nobles, or what was left of them, swear allegiance to his daughter Matilda, that she would be queen of England after his death, it did not quite happen how he hoped.

With these questions over his succession, Henry grew anxious and paranoid. He had, after all, already survived an assassination attempt by one of his own daughters. Juliane went for Henry with a crossbow because he had blinded two of her daughters, his own granddaughters. This sacrifice was in payment for the blinding of another child who was in his custody. Now, worried for his life, Henry would move beds often and he increased the royal guard around him. He slept with a sword and shield nearby and frequently had nightmares of being set upon. Despite his paranoia, or maybe because of it, Henry reigned for longer than any previous English king.

Henry was sixty-seven years old in November of 1135. He was

reasonably fit for this age, though he had grown a little fatter. He had been out hunting and it was time for a feast. Pass those lampreys, a surfeit of them, if you please. Lampreys are eel-like. They are not actually eels, but it is the easiest way to describe them. They are parasitic, jawless fish that attach themselves to other fish like salmon and trout. Let's be honest, you would probably rather eat the salmon, but Henry had other ideas. A surfeit of lampreys is a lot of them. So many that this story is told to represent what happens when you keep having too many good things. Punishment awaits the glutton. The story of Henry's death is intended to suggest that Henry brought this on himself, through foolish overindulgence and gluttony. He ignored the advice of his doctors, or so they made sure to say to distance themselves from his death. He knocked those lampreys back anyway, lots of them.

It is most likely that salmonella or another such bacteria was passed via the fish to the King's gut. Henry would have felt the onset of infection with stomach cramps, diarrhoea that could have been bloody, and fevers, nausea, vomiting, chills and head-ache. It can manifest within a few hours or can even take a few days. When looking at your plate piled high with lampreys, you can't see, smell or taste salmonella bacteria. Servants or animals living around Henry could have carried the salmonella bacteria in their intestines and expelled them in their faeces, spreading it to foods the servants might handle. Or even the familiar handshake from an infected friend could have done it.

The surgeon Clifford Brewer, in his book *The Death of Kings*, argues that the King fell ill far too soon after eating the lampreys.

Infection, he said, would have taken much longer to manifest. He suggested it was more likely an immediate illness brought on by the perforation of a gastric ulcer perhaps, leading to peritonitis, which would account for the fever and vomiting. He would not expect a build-up of salmonella to be as rapid if it caused the King's downfall. An infection with salmonella can however manifest symptoms within a few hours, and the symptoms of abdominal pain, diarrhoea and fever can suggest a few possible diagnoses. Of course, the surgeon might well be simply seeing a surgical problem and a physician an infection with which he is more familiar. One could argue either way. In any case, Henry I died on 1 December 1135. He was sixty-seven years old.

That was not the end of Henry's story though. Of course not. After his death, his body had quite a trip. Henry had asked that he be buried at Reading Abbey, which he himself had founded. He had paid the monks there to pray for his father's soul and for the salvation of his own. Reading Abbey became a magnificent church and religious community, one of the largest monasteries in Europe. The abbey is a ruin now. It can be found in the centre of the town of Reading in the English county of Berkshire. Why Reading? Chronicler William of Malmesbury tells us it was strategic geographically – 'A place calculated for the reception of almost all who might have occasion to travel to more populous cities in England'. The problem with being buried at Reading was that Henry died on the other side of the English Channel. It was not going to be easy to get him back to England before things started to turn sour. Henry's body needed a good embalmer.

First, they took out his intestines, which were then buried

nearby at the priory at Notre Dame du Pré in Rouen. Despite removal of the intestines, which if not taken out can cause trouble quickly in the dead, Henry started to smell bad. The man given the task of removing the brain supposedly collapsed due to the grimness of the task. They rubbed Henry's insides with a scented balm, and they covered him in ox hides.

Onwards to the coast then, but the December weather was terrible and for four weeks they could not sail across the Channel. During that time, putrefaction took over the King's body. Stinking black juices started to spill onto the floor below. The commentary of decay, so vivid in the descriptions of the deaths of both Henry I and his father William I, wonderfully gruesome stories as they are to tell, should not be taken at face value. They represent so much more than simply trying to put us off our breakfast. They tell us exactly how the kings in question were thought of and how the writers of these stories wanted them to be remembered. Christians believed that a deceased person's body resists decay. Such stinking, revolting putrefaction suggests moral corruption and a fate that their bodies deserved in death. Make no mistake: this is how the chroniclers wanted us to remember these men.

What was left of Henry's dripping corpse was laid to rest at Reading Abbey. He lay undisturbed for 400 years until the doors of the abbey were closed on the orders of Henry VIII. The monks were sent packing, the abbot was executed, the valuable possessions were taken by Henry VIII. The burial place of Henry I, who was interred in front of the high altar, was left in ruins. Whatever parts of Henry I made it back from Normandy are somewhere under the site of a Victorian prison known well to Oscar Wilde, or maybe we have another 'King under a car park' as Richard III had become known. With Henry in the ground and without a male heir above it, it was intended that his daughter Matilda should rule. Her cousin Stephen had other ideas.

Stephen

Died 1154

'A violent seizure of the bowels'
Sir Richard Baker, author of
A Chronicle of the Kings of England

There's something not quite right about the name King Stephen. It just doesn't roll off the tongue easily. For many, it should never even have been. The name Stephen does mean 'kingly' so, let's just call him Stephen. Stephen was king despite the Anglo-Norman barons swearing allegiance to the Empress Matilda, daughter of Henry I. He was even one of those on bended knee, swearing to stand by Henry's daughter as queen. Once Henry was dead and buried though, he took the throne for himself. He was a man after all, and he was popular in court. He was well known, wealthy and had a strong history of loyal support for Henry I, just not his daughter. Not only would having a woman on the throne have been unprecedented, but Matilda had not even been around. She had lived in Europe for years as she had been married young to the Holy Roman Emperor, Henry V. Worse still, she was later married to a chap nobody liked much, Geoffrey of Anjou. It was inevitable that a man should fill in, and up stepped Cousin Stephen.

Stephen was the grandson of William the Conqueror, but he was not the son of his predecessor Henry I, whose only surviving heir was his daughter Matilda. She was snubbed for the throne in favour of the cousin by those nobles not wanting a woman in power. Matilda really did not take it well, so she decided to fight, and what followed was years of civil war known as the Anarchy. At the end of it all, Stephen kept hold of the crown.

When it came to Stephen's succession, yet again it was not simple. His eldest son Eustace died in 1153. Accused of violating the shrine of St Edmund, contemporary commentators said Eustace deserved to be struck down suddenly at the age of twenty-three. We don't know what he died of, except maybe the wrath of God for plundering Church lands. Stephen took it badly, but he did calm down and think more favourably of peace. Once again, a king was left having to think long and hard about who his successor might be. In the 1153 Treaty of Wallingford, Stephen and Henry, Matilda's son, made a deal that Stephen would reign until he was dead and then Henry would take over as king. Henry did not have to wait long: the following year Stephen fell ill.

King Stephen is recorded as having died of apoplexy, though not the apoplexy that we might think of. A word no longer used in medical notes, it has changed meaning over the centuries. In the nineteenth century it became a name used to describe the illness brought on by stroke. That could be from a clot to the brain, but also from a bleed. Originally, however, apoplexy referred to bleeding into any internal organ, and in Stephen's case it was bleeding into his gut. He had a disease in his bowel which meant that his blood was leaching out *per rectum*. It would have been a painful way to go for the King.

We think of an exsanguination, a bleeding out, as being associated with traumatic injury or the rupture of a major blood vessel from an aneurysm. Severe, life-threatening blood loss can occur from the gut too. Constant unchecked oozing, without surgery to stem the flow, also kills. The gut is well supplied with blood vessels. Ulcerations of the vessel walls can occur in the presence of infection and suppuration. They rupture and leak blood into the surrounding tissue and out of the rear end.

When blood starts to flow out, unchecked, a healthy, fit individual without disease of the heart or lungs, might be able to compensate for the blood loss for a while. The number of breaths he takes in every minute starts to rise, and Stephen may not even have noticed at first. His heart rate too would have increased, and the stroke volume – the amount of blood pushed out with each squeeze of the heart's ventricles – also rose.

Stephen felt cold. One of the most common symptoms of exsanguination is hypothermia. Blood poured from his bowel, probably dripping down onto the toes of any attendant at his bedside. As the remaining blood was redistributed by the body, the attendants may have noticed their monarch's hands becoming a dark, dusky grey-purple colour. When his friend, Prior Ralph of Holy Trinity arrived to attend to the dying king, his nostrils would have been filled with the distinctive stench of blood loss from the bowel, mixed with the kingly faeces. His blood pressure started to drop. When the blood pressure becomes too low, the cerebral cortex is sacrificed first, with the remaining blood favouring the basic, life-sustaining functions of the brain stem, to keep the body going for as long as possible. Stephen, like the rest of us, was an obligate aerobe, needing oxygen for growth. Without oxygen the cells were dying and taking the life of the King with them. Without blood flowing, the cells were not getting the much-needed supply of oxygen, and carbon dioxide levels would have built up. During hypovolaemic shock, sufferers struggle for air, trying to pull in more and more oxygen, but the blood flow becomes inadequate, no matter how fast the sufferer can breathe or pump the remaining blood.

For Stephen there would have been a few, heaving gasps for air, maybe the violent tightening of the laryngeal muscles letting off an alarming barking sound. There was probably a heaving of agonal (gasping) convulsions of the chest or shoulder muscles, and a death rattle let out as the King died.

Richard Baker wrote that 'He was suddenly seized with iliac passion and with an old disease of emroids'. It was a 'violent seizure of the bowels'. Gervase of Canterbury wrote that 'The King was suddenly seized with pain in the iliac region along with an old discharge from haemorrhoids'. Nobody worried about copying each other's work, clearly.

Clifford Brewer, author of the book *The Death of Kings*, ever the surgeon, suggests he died instead of appendicitis, based on the pain Stephen encountered 'in the iliac region'. Appendicitis should be amongst the first diagnostic thoughts of any medic, surgeon or otherwise. The iliac region is low down in the abdomen, left or right. Alas, which side of his abdomen was most painful was not mentioned. Typically for an appendicitis one might feel that pain on the right side of the abdomen. The appendix is a finger-shaped pouch that comes off the colon on the right side of the body. Acute inflammation of the vermiform appendix can be caused by a blockage. That could be of normal stool or a faecolith (a compacted, stony mass of faeces), it could be infection or even lymphoid hyperplasia. The appendix then becomes inflamed, swollen and filled with pus, so much so that it might rupture and spill its contents into the surrounding tissue, the abdominal cavity. There the bacteria are free to eat away, to burp and fart as bacteria like to do in our dead kings, and in turn be gobbled up by immune cells, thus producing more pus. The gathering of pus can turn into an abscess.

Simply to describe pain as iliac does not specify that region enough. Perhaps the haemorrhoid bleeding was merely anal blood loss mistaken for haemorrhoids, as Brewer thought, but it seems strange to me that this noted *per rectum* blood loss would be coincidental. Whatever the disease was, it resulted in the King meeting his maker in 1154 when he was about sixty years old.

Of course, there are more possibilities in the differential diagnosis: diverticulitis and viral gastroenteritis. Abdominal symptoms can signal a baffling number of diseases. Unlike with the death of kings before him, chroniclers did not moralise on the death of Stephen, despite his reign bringing violence and anarchy. He did though, they noted, have time to receive sacraments. To mention such matters was important as it signalled that they thought he deserved to receive them, despite years of civil war under his rule. With succession plans in place and Matilda's son Henry on his way to London, it was a peaceful transition.

King Stephen, his wife Matilda of Boulogne and their son Eustace were all buried together at Faversham Abbey. It was an abbey they had founded themselves and they chose their own burial places. With the dissolution of the monasteries came upheaval once again and all three graves were lost. Like Henry I under Reading Abbey (gaol), their bones are in there somewhere, but nobody knows exactly where.

Henry II

Died 1189

'Shame. Shame on a conquered king.'
Henry II's last words (allegedly!)

There is no surviving Shakespeare play about Henry II. I say no *surviving* play because such subject matter would have made for tremendous storytelling. Shakespeare must surely have been on the case? There have been other playwrights of course who have delved into the rich pickings of Henry's life, his passions and his priest. Much of the commentary on Henry II's life brings up the problematic falling-out with and the killing of his old friend Thomas Becket. Though the Church-versus-monarchy upheaval that led to Becket's murder was a massive part of his thirty-five years on the throne, it overshadows Henry's many achievements, including legal reforms, and improvements for English government and society that are now being appreciated. He was strong willed and a great leader. Henry spoke many languages and was keen to discuss philosophy and history. He was no slouch. The murder of Becket at the swords of Henry's knights became a defining story in his reign, so he cannot take too much glory.

Henry II was the son of the Empress Matilda and Geoffrey of Anjou. As such he was the grandson of Henry I. After the mess of the Anarchy, with its nineteen years of civil war, Henry had to get England back on track. He pulled the kingdom back from the chaotic poverty brought about by the war with the help of his trusted friend, Becket. Henry gave him the job of Archbishop of Canterbury, but the power changed Becket and became more important to him than the King. Becket insisted that the Church was above the law. Henry did not accept this – for him the laws of the royal court were greater than the Church – and so the power struggle continued. 'Will someone rid me of the troublesome priest,' he muttered. Some quote Henry as saying 'turbulent', some say 'meddlesome' – either way, Becket was certainly troublesome. Four knights took the King at his word. They entered the cathedral at Canterbury and brought down the defenceless archbishop. They spilled his brains and blood onto the flagstones before the cathedral altar as he quietly spoke, 'For the name of Jesus and the protection of the Church, I am ready to embrace death.' Henry would later walk barefoot into Canterbury, paying penance at the altar of the cathedral where Becket had been murdered. At least Henry recognised that this was the greatest mistake of his reign and he regretted it for the rest of his life.

Henry II was married to the powerhouse Eleanor of Aquitaine, whom he had married within two months of her divorce from the dull monk-like French king Louis VII. Married to the king of

France, Eleanor had no heir, but now married to Henry, King of England, they had eight children.

In 1170, in a scene reminiscent of his grandfather's *White Ship* disaster, Henry II survived a storm in which five ships were sunk, taking many nobles with them. Four hundred lives were lost in the sinking, freezing and drowning. They were on their way to crown Henry's fifteen-year-old son, also called Henry, as the Young King, to ensure succession. It was the tradition of the French to crown the young heirs while the father still lived. This time the heir to the throne survived the sinking ship disaster. Henry the Young King was well liked, owing much to his love of tournaments and chivalry, but he did not show much interest in the family business of government. Henry the Young King never lived long enough to enjoy the throne in his own right. He died of dysentery whilst on campaign near Limoges, but not before falling out with his father for denying him meaningful power of his own. He was only twenty-eight years old.

A few months after the Young King's coronation ceremony, old Henry grew sick. So sick that many believed him to have died. Henry's mood was always up and down, this way and that. He suffered a mental illness thought perhaps to be bipolar disorder. For some it was merely the passion of the Plantagenets. He was the first of the Plantagenet kings and his possible bipolar condition became a familial issue that haunted him and his descendants. Henry was always on the move, never stopping. It was said that he liked to keep everyone guessing. He made arrangements to meet people early and then would turn up late. He said one thing and did another entirely.

Henry's sons, who felt hard done by without lands or power of their own, were becoming thorns in his side. They turned against him for want of more power, and they turned on each other. In 1173 Eleanor, who was also fed up with Henry, was caught, disguised as a man, while trying to get to her sons in France. She was imprisoned, put on house arrest by her own husband.

While arguing and fighting continued to rage with his sons, Henry started to look gaunt. He developed a lingering fever and became acutely depressed. Fever, or pyrexia, is often accompanied by lethargy, loss of appetite and depression. Henry suffered from these too. The energy of his youth diminished, Henry's fever was a sign that his body was probably trying to fight off an infection, be it viral, bacterial or even parasitic. Fevers are most associated with infections, but they can indicate some other pathology, such as another chronic inflammatory disorder. Within Henry's brain, compensatory and complementary processes were set in motion, to fight off the invader. The optimal temperature for biochemical processes within the body is 37°C. A fever is defined loosely as the body's core temperature rising above 38°C. It is a useful mechanism, but if the temperature runs too high, organ damage can occur. When the temperature is raised, heat shock proteins are produced. These heat shock proteins stimulate and aid lymphocytes, the white blood cells, the cells of the immune system. Henry's body was trying to fight something off, but what it was, we don't know.

In 1189 Henry was defeated on the battlefield by his son Richard while his body was being defeated by whatever was within him. He withdrew to Chinon where he died in delirium.

His death had been attributed to blood poisoning – an idea extrapolated from the reports that Henry suffered from a persistent fever. It would need to be an agent that was prone to hanging around, like a malarial infection, as he was ill with fevers for some time. Matthew of Westminster wrote that 'Henry plunged into the depths of despair, cursing the day that he was born, ended his life at Chinon on July 6th.' He was supposed to have said the famous last words, 'Shame. Shame on a conquered king.' That would have been quite impressive – if he was indeed delirious he would not have been able to construct the thoughts needed to say such a thing. Shakespeare would probably have made much more of it.

Henry died in the heartlands of the Plantagenets, and his body was not transported to England like that of his grandfather Henry I. Nobody wanted to see dripping putrefied kingly juices again. He was interred at Fontevraud Abbey in Anjou with the Young King, later to be joined by his son Richard, but first Richard had some kingly matters of his own to attend to.

Eleanor of Aquitaine

Died 1204

The death of Eleanor of Aquitaine, despite her being a powerhouse, was not mentioned as much as her husband's or son's demise. She retired to the abbey at Fontevraud, and was eighty-two years old when she died. There were no mentions of delirium or fever, no bodily explosions, or the drippings of rotting flesh. She did not die at the head of an army in battle or of gushing dysentery in an army camp.

Medieval queens were seen as passive diplomacy pieces in the game of thrones. There was no need to tell stories about their death that would function as a comment on their lives or morals. Queens were simply written out of stories, not mentioned unless their deaths left their husbands without an heir. There was no real need for chroniclers to make political statements about the deaths of queens, but more was made of how the kings mourned. It was all about them. Historians are now rightly reassessing the roles of the unjustly forgotten queens, gaining respect for long forgotten acts and involvement. They played much greater roles than was admitted by the contemporary chroniclers.

Eleanor was buried at Fontevraud. Her bones were later scattered when the tombs were vandalised during the French Revolution.

Richard I

Died 1199

The Lion by the ant was slain.

Richard I spent most of his life fighting in France and did not achieve a great deal for England. That he remains a hero of English history is testament to his rather successful 800-year-old marketing department, who point out that even being nowhere to be seen was marginally better than the contribution made by his useless and disliked brother, John. Unlike his brothers, Richard grew up in France, a favourite at the court of his mother Eleanor of Aquitaine at Poitou. He was well educated, both in the classroom and at the arts of fighting and chivalry. He was first made a knight by the king of France, Philip II, and he grew up with a fabulous reputation as a soldier and leader. His nickname was Richard Coeur de Lion: Richard the Lionheart.

Richard's brothers had grown up in the court of their father Henry II. The sons of Henry II were not on good speaking terms with each other or with their father, so Richard joined with his brother John and the king of France in rebelling against Henry II. In his youth and in this reign, Richard's relationships jumped from swings to roundabouts.

Richard had two older brothers. The first-born, William, had died young. Primogeniture (the first-born son automatically becoming heir) was not yet a thing with the Angevins, so when his next older brother Henry died, Richard did not, as a matter of course, become the heir apparent to his father's crown. When Henry II died, only Richard and his younger brother John remained, but Richard was in France, and his brother wasn't. The crown of England was there for Richard's taking. After his coronation in 1189 he released his mother from captivity (she too had fallen out with her husband Henry II and was imprisoned). He declared Arthur, the son of his late brother Geoffrey of Anjou, his heir, and with that done, he headed off to fight. Who knows what it was that Richard did not like about cold, damp, rainy England? He did not hang about in its green fields for long.

Richard's life had all the plot points of a warrior knight's adventure story. Earlier in his youth, he was suspected of making love-not-war with Philip, the king of France. Now, a mission to the Holy Land was led by the pair, along with Leopold of Austria. The third crusade was an assault on the Muslim leader Saladin, who had taken what were then Christian lands, but Richard and his crusaders did not manage to take Jerusalem. Nonetheless it is perhaps the most famous crusade and is considered a successful one. But trouble soon started among Richard's old fraternity. He fell out with Leopold over his claim to the spoils of war – Richard refused Leopold any of the winnings. The stale relationship was rather unfortunate for Richard, as when he was later shipwrecked, he happened to be in Leopold's territory. The King was captured and held for ransom. He also squabbled with his old friend Philip of France, and he fell out with Germany too. They all wanted revenge and to use his capture to demand a huge ransom from England.

Up stood Richard's formidable mother. In a twelfth-century version of running onto the football pitch to defend her son from a vicious tackle, Eleanor of Aquitaine wrote to the Pope. She had strong words with him about Leopold's behaviour. It eventually lead to Leopold's excommunication, so 1–0 to Eleanor, but the massive ransom still had to be paid to get her son back. The money was raised in England, and so much was needed that the coins had to be held in the vault of St Paul's Cathedral, before being taken by Eleanor herself to Europe to ensure the release of her son. Once back in England Richard was symbolically crowned again, and then immediately he headed off to fight, again.

In 1199, while besieging the castle of Chalus in Limousines, Richard was hit by the crossbow bolt that would bring about his end. Passing close to the castle walls with no armour, Richard was a soft target. Bertrand de Gourdon (or maybe his name was Pierre, or John, or Dave – reports differ) had been waiting for the opportunity to get at the King, claiming that his father and two of his brothers had been killed by him. Now his chance had come. A defender on the castle walls was amusing onlookers by jumping about and deflecting English arrows with a frying pan for a shield. Richard was amused, until he was hit in the shoulder.

Accounts differ on which of Richard's shoulders was struck by the crossbow bolt. At first the King did not say anything, not wanting to cause alarm. Back at his tent it became clear that the bolt was embedded so far down into the chest wall that the physicians could not remove the head. They could only dislodge the part of the wooden shaft that had not burrowed deep into the King's body.

Eleven days after being wounded by the bolt, Richard I died from a gangrenous wound. Matthew Paris wrote in *Chronica Majora*, 'a kind of blackness mingled with the swelling, discolouring the region of the wound on every side; this began to give the King intense pain.' His description certainly has a whiff of the gangrene about it. Gas gangrene can be caused by bacteria, most commonly Clostridium perfringens. The gases they give off can kill the surrounding tissues. There may well have been a grisly local infection caused by other bacteria, but this description of blackened skin has meant that gangrene is often quoted as the cause of Richard the Lionheart's long, drawn-out death. It would have started with the skin looking pale, before alarmingly beginning to turn purple. The skin could even have become bubbly in texture, with gas gathering below the surface, turning the King's chest wall into purple-blackened painful bubble wrap. With this description, and Richard's death ten or eleven days after the injury, it is likely that sepsis took the King's life.

Previously known as septicaemia, blood poisoning or septic shock, sepsis is a syndrome of multi-organ failure brought about by infection and the body's response to it. The metal head of the crossbow bolt would have taken in dirt and bacteria, and maybe even small dirty rags of the clothing that it had ripped through, on the way. This warm mixture within his moist body would provide a perfect breeding ground for germs to quickly multiply and cause Richard's lungs, liver, kidneys and brain to fail.

Death from sepsis follows a predictable pattern of events. Richard would at first have a fever. He might be feeling hot or very cold and shivery. Raising temperature is a response of the body to try to slow down the physiological workings of the bacteria as well as setting off a cascade of immune responses. The fever is accompanied by pain and nausea. His pulse would have quickened, and he would have started to breath faster. These responses to the infection are designed to help oxygen get where it is needed, but Richard's blood pressure would have dropped because the chemicals released affect the blood vessels, reducing their resistance and allowing blood to pool. It was not a good position for the King to be in.

One of the first systems to be noticeably affected by all of this is the respiratory or breathing system. The lungs can develop pulmonary oedema as the small blood vessels leak unwanted fluid that gathers to affect the transfer of oxygen across the lung tissue. An X-ray of Richard's chest might show the fluid as white shadows across the normally dark, air-filled lung fields. As the blood is not oxygenated as readily, his oxygen levels would have started to drop. In severe sepsis, with blood and oxygen not getting to where they're needed, lactate (a product of the cells needed to produce energy without any oxygen) builds up and carbon dioxide levels alter, driving the respiratory response. The acute respiratory distress would have been noticeable in Richard as he lay on his deathbed gasping for air.

If we could have taken a much closer look at Richard's blood, we'd see an increase in the white blood cells as his immune system tried to mobilise a defence. There would be a surge in the production and output of the proteins involved in immunity such as C-reactive protein (CRP). CRP is a protein made by the liver in response to immune cells secreting their signalling molecules. CRP binds to dead or dying cells, flagging them up, in order to activate the immune system's complement pathway (the cascade of factors that amplify and enhance immune cells and antibodies). So, when there is a problem requiring an immune response, CRP levels escalate and this rise can be detected in the blood, as a marker of inflammation.

When the liver fails due to the lack of oxygen and other nourishment, it struggles to make these much-needed molecules. The biochemical knock-on effect is widespread. The disruption of blood clotting, for instance, controlled in part by formation of the clotting factors by the liver, can be disastrous. Epithelial cells that line the intestines and the stomach can be destroyed, leading to ulcers and bleeding from the gut, worsened by the ongoing problem with clotting.

When there is a reduction in blood flow to the kidneys, they can no longer remove the toxins that they normally filter from the blood, and the kidneys themselves become damaged. Less urine is produced and there follows a developing uraemia as the waste product urea builds up in the blood. Electrolyte imbalances occur when the kidneys are not functioning properly, and loss of some electrolytes, or the build-up of others, can affect muscle, particularly the cardiac muscle, causing fibrillations of the heart.

Richard I

When blood flow and oxygen supply to the brain is diminished there could be irritability and agitation, delirium and confusion. This would have come at the end for the forty-one-year-old king.

Richard I died on 6 April 1199 with his mother by his side. 'The Lion by the ant was slain' became a popular phrase. The mighty king had been brought down by the lowly crossbowman. It could equally be used to reference the tiny bacterial invader that killed the mighty king with an overwhelming infection. Some believe that Bertrand was summoned by the King to his deathbed and was pardoned for his part in it, even given coins. The dying did have a habit of asking for and handing out forgiveness as a last-minute hedging of bets before reckoning with their maker. Others believe that whilst the pardon might have helped the dying Richard, it did not do Bertrand any good. After Richard's death, Mercardier, the leader of the infamous brutal mercenaries the Brabacons, ordered that the young perpetrator be flayed alive.

Next came the task of deciding what to do with the King's remains. Richard's lion heart, his entrails and his body were all buried in separate places. His bowels, organs and brain were buried in Limoges, and his body was taken to Fontevraud Abbey to lie at the feet of his father Henry II. His heart was taken out, embalmed, and put in its own little lead box to be buried at Rouen. Dug up hundreds of years later and analysed in 2013, it was found they had embalmed it in myrtle, daisy, mint and lime. It sounds like they were preparing it for the frying pan rather than a lead coffin.

The practice of separating out the heart of a king in this manner, and giving him a special send-off, probably came from the Crusades. Soldiers and nobles were far from home and if they died, they did not want their bodies to stay in what they considered to be this undesirable, heathen place. Sending a whole dead body all the way back to England, though, was somewhat tricky. So, the heart came out and was sent home to the family with ceremony. The heart burials became symbolic, especially for the kings who were thought to have been chosen by God. The kings, queens and nobles would ask for their hearts to be buried in a particular place that held special meaning to them – much as we scatter ashes today. Their body might also be buried in a place that was special to the kingdom to spread the symbolism. Notably, no part of Richard's body was sent to England.

Entrails are full of faecal matter and bacteria, and the mechanisms that keep those stinky matters apart from the rest of the body in life, break down in death. The gut bacteria are free to spread out and go to lunch. They putrefy the body a lot faster, so back in Richard's day they needed to whip those out and bury them close to where the person died, if their body were to have a long final journey. Like Henry I's last trip back to England, it was a messy business. The local monks were supposedly not too impressed at being left with Richard's entrails. To them, the filthy innards signified all the badness in the man, and the monks would rather not have had to handle that, even if they were from a king.

In 1191, eight years before his death, Richard had married Berengaria of Navarre, but the couple mostly lived well apart. Richard had no children, legitimate or otherwise (another reason for historians to question his sexuality). As he had no heir, Richard requested that Arthur would be crowned king. Richard's brother John had other ideas. Not long after, Arthur was murdered.

John

Died 1216

'Foul as it is, hell itself is defiled by the fouler presence of John.'
Attributed to Matthew Paris, St Alban's Abbey chronicler

King John was hated then and he is still hated now. He was intimidating, cowardly and sadistic. We love to hate King John as much as we love to love his brother Richard. They are remembered very differently. Few have anything nice to say about John. Kate Norgate, biographer of King John, in 1902 described him as a man of 'almost superhuman wickedness'. Later scholars questioned his mental health, in a similar way questioning his father's case of the passion of the Plantagenets. Though some have tried to be sympathetic to John, there does not seem to be such a large appetite for his rehabilitation, as we see with Richard III.

When King John died, in October of 1216, he had succumbed to dysentery. A fitting termination, some might say, for this greedy, self-serving man to end with foul diarrhoea spewing uncontrollably from his bowels, taking his life with it. John may not have been dispatched by an unhappy crowd, but it was good timing for his disgruntled subjects.

Being the fourth son of Henry II, young John was not very likely to become king. There was no rule of primogeniture yet, that made the first-born male automatically become the heir, but loyalties between the various sons were divided. Even John's parents, Henry and Eleanor, argued over who was their favourite son. John was even called Lackland, as there were no lands of the Angevin Empire given to the fourth-born son. But that was not going to stop the jealous, bitter young man from trying. Richard became the next king of England, but his death in 1199 brought about the question of succession once again.

John's nephew, twelve-year-old Arthur, Duke of Brittany and son of his brother Geoffrey, was favoured to be king after gangrene got the better of Richard I. The young man stood between John and the crown. John captured Arthur and then, he conveniently just disappeared. Some stories even have it that Arthur was murdered by John's own hand.

At first John ordered that the lad be rendered useless to the kingdom by blinding and castration. Those sent to carry out the deed could not bring themselves to do it and so Arthur was taken from his chains at the castle at Rouen and led down to the river to meet his uncle. John himself put a dagger through the boy's heart and threw his limp body into the river, weighted down with rocks.

With his older brothers now dead and having wickedly dispatched his young nephew Arthur, John was able to claim the throne. His reign was marred by the rumoured treatment of Arthur, and by his terrible decisions to come. Of course, the stories about his murder of Arthur may have been embellished to help the cause against the King, but Arthur had disappeared, and somebody had to have killed him. John was the obvious candidate.

At thirty-two years old, John had taken his chance, but he very soon became known as The Bad King. He was so bad that his barons united against their monarch, demanding their rights be restored. They forced him to sign the Magna Carta at Runnymede in 1215. It is one of the most significant documents in English history, acknowledging baronial rights, protecting them from illegal imprisonment and limiting feudal payments to John and the Crown. Magna Carta allowed the barons the right to hold the ruler to account. As pub quiz trivia goes, Magna Carta in 1215 comes up all the time. This is a sure point for our team.

The atmosphere during John's reign was so toxic that many believed the end of the world to be nigh, but fortunately the world did not end as predicted in 1212. John even managed to get the Pope to absolve him of the promises made in the Magna Carta not long after he signed it.

Unbelievably, the disgruntled nobles even offered the throne to the French Prince Louis. Considering that hundreds of years of strife had passed between the nations, it is amazing that the English would ask the French king to take over. Things must have been truly bad. Unopposed, Louis landed in England and was installed as king. John, slightly annoyed, gathered men in Yorkshire and Lincolnshire in the north and headed south to face the rebels. His trip was a disaster though, and John is oft remembered for losing the King's treasures. His baggage train was caught by rising waters and went down in the tidal estuary of the Wash.

After that calamitous day followed an evening of gluttony, when John feasted on fruits and cider, and soon he developed a sudden onset of abdominal pain and a fever. With his stomach cramping painfully and with the fever muddling his thoughts, he had a sleepless, sweat-filled night. The next day, still in pain, fevered and exhausted, he could not even mount his horse. He had to be carried between castles over the next couple of days and on the fourth day, weakened, dehydrated and overcome with the infection, he died at Newark.

Once again, the story of a king's death was symbolically significant. John's dysentery was fitting, and it was believed that the sin of greed and gluttony had led to his downfall. To die like this reflected his military record of defeat and his weakening of the English claims to Normandy as well as his terrible treatment of his people. He was another repressor of the Church and as such, his painful, foul death was interpreted as fitting and deserved.

The whole sorry event could not have passed by without at least an eyebrow raised. Nobody would be surprised if John had indeed been offered a poisoned chalice by an unhappy monk, but his death was recorded as dysentery and that was probably quite helpful to those who followed in his royal footsteps.

In this time, before the assumption that monarchs would be buried at Westminster Abbey, King John was buried at Worcester Cathedral. That was a bit of a trek across the country from Newark to Worcester with a stinking body that had died of a gushing bowel disease.

John

Kings were laid to rest in places all over the land, with William II at Winchester, Henry I at Reading and Henry II at Fontevraud in Anjou with his other son, Richard I. John had requested to be buried at the cathedral at Worcester, reflecting his devotion to the saints Dunstan and Wulfstan. St Wulfstan had been a bishop at Worcester, the last surviving pre-Conquest bishop, who was canonised during John's reign by Pope Innocent III. That same pope had excommunicated the king of England, but let's just let bygones be bygones.

Whilst John's body was being taken across country for burial, the barons quickly had to withdraw the acclamation that the Frenchman Louis was king of England. Oh, sorry about that, we made a mistake, back you go to France then, *au revoir*. À *bientôt*.

King John's body managed to lie undisturbed in Worcester for a few hundred years until the reign of George III, when in 1797 there was a dispute about where exactly the coffin was in the church. A tomb or two were opened, just to find out. The Georgians did not need much of an excuse. Shall we open up another coffin?

They found the king that they were looking for. They described that he was 5 foot 6 and a half inches tall. Or should we say long rather than tall, at this point? His body had been shrouded in a monk's cowl, attempting to represent his piousness and an aid to his passage through Purgatory. It sounds like John needed all the help he could get.

The remains of a sword and scabbard lay next to the king's body. Thousands of people flocked to take a peek at the remains before they closed up the tomb again. You would have gone to see it, wouldn't you? As you missed the chance to see the rotten corpse, you can read an account of the opening of King John's coffin at the British Library.

'Vain, capricious, and troublesome' could easily have been used to describe John, but these words were used about his wife, Isabella of Angoulême. When John died, Isabella left her son in the capable hands of William Marshal and returned to France. There she married again and attempted to poison Louis XIV, following an argument with his wife. Isabella fled to Fontevraud Abbey and became yet another queen of England who simply died, without description. The original will and testament of her first husband King John survives at Worcester Cathedral, and is the earliest single-sheet original testament of a royal known to exist from 800 years ago. The crown passed to their nine-year-old son Henry.

Henry III

Died 1272

The third Henry to be king of England was the son of Bad King John. He was only a boy when his father died of dysentery in 1216, and of course he could not rule or make important decisions affecting the kingdom, but a regent could. Being able to control the new king was a good position for some of the barons to be in. The knight William Marshal, with a small group of loyal barons, became regent to young Henry. Louis was sent packing back to France, having been told that they were 'only joking' and that he had never in fact been a king of England. William Marshal reissued Magna Carta and ensured Henry III upheld the promises made in the Grand Charter. The barons did not all sing from the same song sheet though and it spelled trouble for Henry.

Even when he grew to manhood, Henry was a bit useless. He could not get his head around ruling and his finances were a mystery to him. Henry's wife, Eleanor of Provence, took advantage. She sneakily sent Henry's money to her family courts in

France. In England, unsurprisingly, the unrest continued. The rebel Simon de Montfort became committed to the reform of government, and civil war ensued. After defeat at the Battle of Lewes in 1264, Henry was taken prisoner. Simon created a new government and summoned barons and bishops to a parliament with representatives from the boroughs. This was not a true representation of all the land, but the beginning of the tyranny of Simon de Montfort.

Henry managed to get the crown back from de Montfort when his son Edward took down the rebel, defeating him at the Battle of Evesham in 1265. De Montfort's head, complete with his own testicles draped as decoration across his nose, was eventually sent to his grieving widow, Henry's own sister Maud. It was sent the long way round, via different cities of course, for maximum exposure.

Unlike de Montfort, Henry III was spared a traumatic, bloody battlefield death. His was a much slower demise. Henry felt the first sting of a blood clot on the brain when he was in Bury St Edmunds in 1270. He rallied a little but fell ill again and at that point decided that he must be in London, near to his favoured saint, Edward the Confessor (or what was left of him).

Henry then suffered what appeared to be multiple cerebral thromboses – strokes. Little blood clots roamed free through his arteries and became lodged in the vasculature of the brain, blocking the flow of blood.

Blood must flow freely around the vessels to all parts of the body (except the lenses of the eyes). When there is a chance that blood might spill, one needs a fast-acting shut-off mechanism.

Clotting prevents a little cut from becoming a catastrophic exsanguinating disaster and so, blood clots are part of a healthy, normally functioning body. The mechanism is a life-saving necessity, but sadly blood clots can arise and cause trouble where they are not wanted. When this happens, we see heart attacks (myocardial infarctions) or pulmonary embolisms, or as in Henry's case, strokes (cerebrovascular events).

Any damage to a blood vessel triggers the activation of platelets. Platelets, also known as thrombocytes, are colourless little cells in the blood. They stick to the injured vessel walls and clump together to form a plug to seal over the damage, preventing further blood loss. A cascade of blood-clotting factors reacting with each other is set off, recruiting more platelets and more cells, growing the clot. The protein fibrin is there to create a net to catch more platelets and cells, keeping that hole plugged until it can heal.

When the clot has performed its job and the hole has healed enough, the clot will dissolve, leaving the area tidy again, without a gushing breach in the walls. The trigger for the clot formation could have been a simple insult from a paper cut or it could have been from a pathological process inside the vessels themselves. Pathological plaques in blood vessel walls, if they break down, will set off a clotting cascade, sending clots through the vessels. Thromboembolic events, where blood is blocked from getting through, can cause downstream effects in the brain or even death within minutes.

In Henry's brain, the accumulation of multiple small strokes killed him. Each stroke insult might be unnoticed at first, but together there could be cognitive or physical decline that becomes more obvious. With each thrombotic attack on the vasculature of the brain, he became a bit weaker, a bit more confused, a bit less able to function. The nineteenth-century physician William Osler commented on such declines – he said, 'These people take as long to die as they did to grow up.'

Recognised by Osler and described since Hippocrates, we've long understood the symptoms of stroke. A sudden loss of control of one side's limbs, or facial asymmetry or speech problems could be part of the same syndrome. The condition was first referred to as apoplexy. Not until the 1600s, when doctors were carrying out regular autopsies and dissections, did they piece together the signs and symptoms with the clotting or bleeding in the brain.

Henry's accumulation of strokes led to his death in the autumn of 1272. He was sixty-five years old. Having come to the throne so young, and surviving the traumatic battlefield, Henry had the longest reign of all the medieval monarchs, a record he held until George III 500 years later.

Henry had a much-reduced kingdom compared to his predecessors, since his father had lost Normandy and Anjou on the continent. In England he left his mark with the building of impressive cathedrals. The magnificent Wells, York and Lincoln cathedrals all had his assistance.

He also paid handsomely to rebuild Westminster Abbey, carrying the body of Edward the Confessor to a brand-new tomb, and in the Confessor's former resting place, Henry was interred. Like his father, Henry chose to be laid to rest with his favourite saint. He didn't get to stay there for long: Henry's son Edward I created an elaborate tomb for his father and moved him in there.

Edward I

Died 1307

Edward I of England had perhaps the most memorable nickname of any king: he was called Longshanks, on account of his having remarkably long legs. Henry III was only 5 feet 6 inches tall, but his son Edward was 6 feet 2. Along with his fearsome reputation for his ruthless fiery temper and a clear need for anger management classes, his height made him an intimidating figure. He is also remembered as the Hammer of the Scots, though that name came later, long after he was buried beneath his tomb.

Edward grew up ready for a fight in a time of strife as the rebel baron Simon de Montfort was demanding more say in England's rule. He fought against the rebel barons as a warrior prince and, unlike his father, became a warrior king. Edward's reputation for being vindictive and cruel grew with him. When he caught Simon de Montfort, William Wallace and many more, he brutally killed them and displayed their body parts as trophies. Despite how we might think of medieval behaviour, this was not the done thing.

He was not alone in this behaviour though; when William Wallace won at Stirling Bridge, he flayed the captured English knight Hugh de Cressingham and divided his skin between the victors. Wallace used his share of the skin to make a decorative belt for his sword.

In true warrior knight style, Edward became a renowned crusader. So much so that he also became an assassin's target. One such assassin landed a blow on Edward with a poisoned knife before Edward beat and stabbed the man to death. Edward's wife, Eleanor of Castille, is given credit for saving his life by sucking the poison from his wound before the worst could happen. Edward thought highly of his wife anyway and he definitely thought a lot more of her now. Their marriage is remembered fondly as unusually for royals it was a love match as much as a political one. When she died in 1290, Edward was heartbroken. Once again, little was reported of how the Queen died, but plenty was said about how she was mourned by the King. A line of commemorative crosses that mark Eleanor's final journey after her death near Lincoln, to her resting place in London can be traced down through the country. At each point where they stopped for the night, he had a cross erected in her name. Some were built in stone and others remain only in name; Charing Cross, for instance, was the site of an Eleanor cross in London.

Back from the Crusades and crowned king, Edward went west to Wales to take on Llywelyn, the Prince of Wales, who was refusing to pay homage, and there Edward slaughtered his way to victory. After a massive castle-building project provided security in Wales, he turned his interests north, to take on the Scots. When in 1286 Alexander III, King of Scots, accidentally rode his horse off a cliff in a storm, breaking his neck in the process, he left a child, Margaret, as his heir. Edward decided that young Margaret should be married to his own son, uniting the kingdoms, but Margaret died before a crown could touch her head. Nothing went to plan for Longshanks.

The well-organised English army were crossing Stirling Bridge when William Wallace and his men attacked early, cutting a section of them off from the main body of the army. The few who got across the bridge were heading towards soft, difficult terrain. Cut down, bloodied and humiliated, the rest fled.

In 1307 Edward was on his way north to try once again to have words with the Scots, now led by Robert the Bruce. The English got as far as Burgh by Sands, near Carlisle, but Edward did not get any further or see through his quest to defeat the Scots. That familiar feeling rose in his guts. Edward was sick and there was not much that could be done about it.

Once again a mortal monarch died of the painful, messy disease of dysentery, the gut infection strong enough to disable, dehydrate and kill. Edward met the same end as King John. It is easy to imagine that John might have been murdered and Edward could have died in battle. Instead both were brought down and humbled by bloody diarrhoea. Edward knew this was a bad case, he knew he was dying. He asked that his bones be kept as relics, to be carried before any English army heading into battle against the Scots so that he might witness English supremacy over those north of the border. The Scots had other ideas and so did Edward II. Edward's remains were taken south instead to Westminster Abbey, where the remains of his father were waiting for him. Perhaps if Edward's son and heir had been more of a warrior like his father, he might have carried out his wishes and boiled his father in a big pot of king soup to clean up his bones. As it happened, neither Edward nor his son were able to take the crown north of the border.

Perhaps the English rugby team could try. Perhaps they could do with old Edward's bones carried before them as they run onto the pitch at Murrayfield every other year, to the skirl of the pipes and the ferocious sound of thousands of Scotland supporters baying for English blood. They will find Longshanks's bones at Westminster still, and they would not be the first people to go digging there since he was interred 700 years ago.

No monarch interred at Westminster Abbey was going to be safe from prying eyes with inquisitive Georgians about. In 1774 the Society of Antiquaries opened the tomb of Edward I for a look, with permission from the Dean of Westminster. They found Longshanks in red and gold royal robes. He held sceptres in both hands. A drawing was made of the remains, luckily by somebody who was quite good with pen and ink. (That someone turned out to be the poet and artist William Blake, who at the time was apprentice to the engraver of the Society of Antiquaries.) The King was remarkably well preserved. They measured him to find he was still 6 feet 2 inches. An account of their findings lets us know that 'some globular substance, possible fleshy part of the eye-balls, was moveable in their sockets.'

With Edward I interred at Westminster Abbey, very slowly decaying and with no further say in the affairs of England, Wales or Scotland, his son Edward II was free to unleash more drama.

Edward II

Died 1327

You have been waiting for the death of Edward II, haven't you?
Or maybe you couldn't wait? Maybe you came straight to this
one, we see you. The story of the death of Edward II is the stuff
of legend and is as well known as the beheading of Charles I, as
a popular story of grim regicide. To some, this disappointing son
of the mighty warrior King Edward I got what he deserved. However, everything is not quite as it first appears with Edward's death
story. Seven hundred years of stories, revisions, speculation and
embellishment have left us none the wiser about the real truth.

Edward was born in Wales in 1284 at Caernarfon Castle and
was given the title of Prince of Wales at sixteen. There was so
much hope for the prince. He was the fourth son, but his three
older brothers had died young, leaving Edward as heir apparent.
He was a handsome young man, but he became a disappointment
to those around him, including his father. Young Edward was
not interested in the noble art of knighthood and the pastimes

that defined kingliness and fighting men. Instead, he was more interested in outdoor pursuits and the arts, artisan activities, music and plays – and other young men.

Edward's favoured friend, or 'favourite' was Piers Gaveston. He was brought into the prince's household by the King to motivate the prince towards great things. It was a decision Edward I would come to regret. Gaveston was proud and playful but also arrogant. His relationship with the Prince of Wales was so problematic it led to fisticuffs between father and son and between prince and nobles. In one regrettable episode, old Edward, in a display of his famous anger, held Prince Edward down and pulled out clumps of his hair. He then banished Gaveston from the kingdom. Not long after, the death of Edward I meant the new king, Edward II, could bring his friend back from exile.

Gaveston continued to be good-looking, clever, egotistical – and massively annoying. He was especially annoying to other nobles. He liked to make up funny nicknames for them and unsurprisingly they did not like that much. The King showered Gaveston with gifts, land and titles, until eventually the nobles decided that something had to be done.

In June 1312 Gaveston was kidnapped by Guy Beauchamp, the Earl of Warwick, and dragged off to the infamous dungeon at Warwick Castle. There a death sentence was pronounced by Warwick, and Gaveston was moved to Blacklow Hill, on Lancaster land, to be murdered. The job of finishing him off was given to two bloodthirsty Welshmen. One stabbed him with a sword and the other hacked off his head. They discarded his lifeless body to rot where they had decapitated him. It was left to some monks to retrieve Gaveston's remains, do the good deed and bury the King's friend. Today a monument stands on the site where Gaveston was murdered, a Victorian addition to the story. But it was not Edward's only frowned-upon relationship. Hugh Despenser the younger was also implicated, and he too was brutally put to death, this time by hanging, drawing and quartering, on the orders of Edward's wife Isabella and Roger Mortimer (more of him later).

Despite his interest in other young men, Edward married Isabella, the sister of Philip IV, king of France, and together they had four children. If Edward made any smart moves, falling out with his queen was not one of them. Nor perhaps was telling people that he carried a knife in case he might see her. Or if he had no weapon that he might crush her between his teeth. There was no love lost between this royal couple.

Over in France, away from Edward, Isabella met English nobles who had been banished, including Roger Mortimer. When their eyes first met across a crowded courtyard was a pivotal moment. Mortimer was in Paris having escaped from the Tower where he had been imprisoned by the King. He and Isabella got together and hatched a plan. There was trouble ahead. There was trouble coming from many directions for Edward.

Up in Scotland, Robert the Bruce was taking back castles that had been held by Edward's father and so in 1314 Edward led an army north to face Bruce. He was defeated and humiliated by the Scots at the Battle of Bannockburn, in sight of the magnificent Stirling Castle. Those not impaled on spikes or trampled to death broke away and fled the ghastly scene. Edward was chased away. Once again the Scots had sent a Plantagenet homeward, to think again. Maybe if Edward had taken his father's bones as relics to witness the fight as he'd been asked to do, they might have summoned some military prowess at Bannockburn.

Edward's reign was a disaster. Having lost in Scotland and Ireland, and hacked off as many with his relationships as his incompetence, Edward II was deposed by Parliament in 1327. Edward's eldest son became Edward III but as he was only fourteen and still getting up far too late and playing games all day, the country was ruled by Isabella and Roger Mortimer. Edward II was held under guard and was moved from castle to castle whilst Edward III ruled, or rather, whilst Queen Isabella and her boyfriend ruled.

Chronicler Geoffrey le Baker wrote that Edward was deliberately kept in terrible and humiliating conditions at Berkley Castle in Gloucestershire. He based his accounts of Edward II's death on what he had he been told by William Bisschop, who was a friend of Thomas Gurney and John Maltravers, who were said to have murdered the King. Le Baker recounted that the deposed king was starved, and surrounded by the rotting corpses of animals in the hope that he would catch a disease and die naturally. If Edward died naturally of the miasma exuding from decaying matter then there would be no need for someone's direct hand in his death. But Edward had a habit of not doing what people wanted, and he did not die on request. As a deposed king, he remained a threat, even under lock and key, and so his days were numbered. Nobody knows for certain the details of Edward's death, but the story much loved by generations of our schoolchildren is horrific.

Edward II

One sure way of murdering the King and getting away with it would be to hold him down under something heavy and insert a burning rod of copper or a red-hot poker up into his insides, via his rectum. It would leave no obvious outward signs of harm. It is a sure way, but not an obvious one. Smothering, for instance, leaves no outward marks either, nor do some poisons.

Let us investigate the idea that the deposed king was dispatched in such a horrific manner. Edward, who was a fit young man without a protracted illness, died instantly, of something aggressive and fast. If this was indeed a hot iron poker, it would not just have perforated the rectum or the bowel, leaving him to die in a protracted state of peritonitis like William the Conqueror. To kill Edward immediately, the thrust of the poker would need to be deep and aggressive enough to cause injury to major blood vessels. To cut through a large blood vessel within the abdomen would mean a sudden gush of a large volume of blood into the abdomen or out of the rectum. This instant and brutal churning of the guts would have been a bloody affair. The blood pressure within the smaller vessels could not be maintained, the brain would shut down from a lack of blood flow and the heart would soon start to fibrillate without blood to maintain its own muscle or blood to pump.

Edward's chilling screams could be heard from beyond the castle walls. This detail does not really support the theory that the murderers wanted no outward evidence. Surely they would muffle any screams as well.

The gruesome story of the hot poker was embellished and retold time and again through the years. It was also used as a commentary by the monastic chroniclers on the consequences of Edward's homosexuality. This symbolic story was a condemnation not just of the 'sin' itself but the disruption that Edward's improper relationships brought to the kingdom.

The real cause of Edward's death will never be known for sure. If he did die in the castle that day it seems more likely that he was asphyxiated in some way that left no mark. Putting the body on display as proof that he was dead was again not as clear cut as at first it seems. Rumours of Edward's escape, his body being switched and of a life lived in exile all circulated. In the nineteenth century, papers were discovered in Italy that gave a detailed account of Edward having escaped. An Italian bishop wrote to Edward III informing him that his father had escaped to the continent, gone to visit the Pope for a bit and then lived there as a hermit. As witness protection programmes go there are worse places to be sent; at least it was not Stirling. He would not have been welcome there, and it rains a lot.

Ian Mortimer, the historian and biographer of the Plantagenet kings, concluded that Edward did not even die that day at Berkeley Castle in 1327, never mind the intimate details of his torturous death. Dates and timings show that had this been the day of the deposed king's death, neither Edward III nor any others of note would have had a chance to identify Edward II's body before it was embalmed. In the 1300s, the embalming process involved covering the whole body and head in cerecloth, obscuring any view of the face. If this was the King and not a substitute body, few would have seen his dead body close up and proved conclusively it was Edward II before the face was permanently obscured. Interestingly, after this date, the faces of the deceased monarchs were no longer covered in cerecloth during the embalming process. Take from that what you will.

In whatever manner Edward was killed, the red-hot poker story, just like King Harold's arrow at Hastings, has become the mainstay of history classes for every British schoolchild – that is until someone on the internet puts them right with a comment that starts 'Well, actually . . .'

Dead or alive, Edward's disastrous reign was over. It was his son who is remembered as the father of the nation.

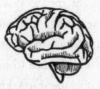

Edward III

Died 1377

'. . . for better or worse, he helped us become what we are.'

Ian Mortimer

To think of Edward III conjures images of a chivalrous Arthurian court, with spectacular tournaments bringing nobles together in training for the great military successes of Edward's reign. Edward is credited with scores of achievements and many believe he was among the best of the kings.

First, he had to break free from the power-hungry Roger Mortimer and when he did, he had Mortimer tried and executed. Hanged, drawn and quartered, Mortimer was given the same brutal treatment he had handed to Hugh Despenser as he casually watched on whilst eating lunch. Edward did not execute his mother, he just locked her up for a bit.

Now able to rule, without his mother and her boyfriend interfering, Edward set about fixing the problems made by his predecessors. He fought the Scots and the French, at one point having both of their kings in custody in England. With Edward having a legitimate claim to the French throne, he started the Hundred Years War with France (though I'm not sure that's what they agreed to call it at the start). He fought outnumbered at Crécy and won an unlikely victory against the French with English longbows destroying their opposition. He won at Poitiers with his son Edward amongst the fray and he also destroyed the French sailing fleet, ensuring that there could not be an attack on England.

He was very much the kingly king of our medieval stories. So, lots of good things happened for England with Edward III on the throne. For some, Edward's reign was marred because he lived far too long. If he had died earlier, in his moment of glory, then things would not have descended into the Wars of the Roses. It was so inconsiderate of him.

Edward sadly descended into senility, which caused him to fall for the bewitching Alice Perrers, his mistress who was lady-in-waiting to his queen, Philippa. Alice does not come off well in the stories of Edward III's last days.

In September 1376 he fell ill with what is described as a large abscess. This diagnosis appears in multiple accounts of the King's life but sadly none give further details. It would be nice to know exactly where Edward's large abscess afflicted him. An abscess is a collection of pus, which itself is a collection of pieces of broken cells, the result of the body defending itself from infectious organisms and trying to contain the debris. There's a big difference between an abscess on a foot or leg and an abscess of the tooth, the parotid gland, or even a peri-anal affliction. As the immune system kicks into action, the area around an abscess can be painful, red, swollen and angry-looking. If it bursts, it spews out the pus. Edward's was painful, and gave off a terrible smell. Credit to one writer who tells us that Edward 'had an abscess on his body' – as helpful an insight as any. It is mentioned more than once that the mystery abscess burst in the month of February, but still no mention of where it burst on his body.

On his sixty-fourth birthday Edward gave gifts of robes to the household physicians and surgeons, all seven of them. They had no staff shortages in that infirmary. The medical men were clearly playing an important role for Edward at that time.

Though the Black Death swept through Europe and Edward's England during his reign, he personally escaped the disease. One third of the population were not so lucky and Edward's family did not escape. His daughter Jeanne succumbed to the plague as she travelled through France to be married in Spain.

One clue about Edward's cause of death was found as recently as the 1940s, after the Second World War. It was a treasure made not of gold but of plaster. Restorers at Westminster Abbey found a death mask inside the head of his wooden effigy. Death masks were made by moulding plaster or wax over the face of the recently deceased to capture their likeness in death. It is a little like the post-mortem death photography of the Victorian era, and just as creepy. Edward's death mask exhibits a distortion, a drooping of the left side of his mouth, suggesting that he suffered a stroke. But a single stroke would not explain the cognitive decline that Edward displayed in his later years. It may be that

Edward III suffered the same fate as Henry III. Multiple smaller strokes over time, leading to cognitive decline and a final, larger, life-ending event in 1377 when he was sixty-four years old.

There are of course differing reasons for cognitive decline. We must recognise that Edward was a Plantagenet, with the genes passed down through the generations, associated with mental ill health. We can only speculate about Edward's death, with the help of a few clues. But we know much more about what Alice Perrers was up to. It was claimed by her enemies that she pulled the rings off his fingers as he lay dying, to line her pockets.

While we don't know much about his death, a description of what happened to Edward's body gives a good picture of embalming practice. First the body was laid out and chamberlains washed him down. He was then rubbed all over, pushing balsam and spices into every fold and orifice. A knife sliced through skin from xiphisternum (the lower part of the breastbone) down the centre of his abdomen to the pubis, and the skin layers and fat were pulled apart, providing enough space to remove the viscera. Omentum (the lining of fat and connective tissue that covers and supports the organs of the abdomen), stomach, intestines, liver . . . all the organs had to come out. The skull was cut open and his brain was pulled out, to be replaced with more oils and spices that would hold back putrefaction. He was then wrapped in layers of waxy cerecloth. Each of the King's fingers and thumbs were wrapped individually in the cloth 'as if the hands were covered in linen gloves'. The sum of £21 was paid to a Roger Chandler for the balsams and oils used to cover Edward's remains. This ritual was not simply to ward off the rotting process, but also to keep the body as pure as possible, in keeping with the intact corpse required for the saintliness.

Edward was then wrapped in a long tunic and a silk handkerchief was placed over his face. A ring was placed on a finger and covered with gloves. A rod with a cross was placed across his chest, the sceptre placed in his left hand.

He was buried at Westminster Abbey with his wife, Philippa. A torchlit procession accompanied his coffin, stopping overnight at St Paul's Cathedral. Over 500 members of the King's household were provided with black mourning uniforms, and 400 torchbearers were given black hooded cloaks to wear in the procession. A gilt-bronze effigy of Edward III can be seen on the marble tomb at Westminster. The head lies upon a pillow given by Queen Victoria. There are twelve decorated figures to represent his children. Believe it or not, the majority of people of English ancestry can expect to be descended from Edward III, and so as Ian Mortimer concludes in his book, *The Perfect King*, '. . . for better or worse, he helped us become what we are.'

The Black Prince

Died 1376

'My beauty great, is all quite gone,
My flesh is wasted to the bone.'
From the tomb of the Black Prince
in Canterbury Cathedral

If we were to devote only one sentence to the death of the Black Prince, it would probably contain the word dysentery, but far more was going on with Prince Edward of Woodstock. He was in and out of a sick bed for years before his final illness. It was not an acute, eat-something-and-die sort of dysentery, it was more prolonged than that. At the Battle of Poitiers in 1356 he believed himself blessed with near supernatural strength. It must have come as a bit of a shock when his bowels started to turn themselves inside out. The Black Prince didn't fear death though – he scorned it.

Edward of Woodstock's reputation is still controversial. Perhaps because he did not live to gain the throne, he was held up on a high pedestal as the mighty warrior that he could have been. For his enemies though, he was seen as a brutal tormenter. His nickname of the Black Prince has a few conflicting origin stories. One reason he might have been given the frightening name comes from the cruelty he inflicted on his enemies, particularly the French at Limoges. Another theory is the warrior Prince favoured black armour. Some say his name came from his tomb, which was made of metal that turned black in the sunlight coming in through the window above his resting place at Canterbury Cathedral.

The sacking of Limoges in September of 1370 was indeed dark, but remember the prince was already sick, weakened and swollen. No one is in a good mood when their insides are turning themselves inside out and swelling up out of all proportion. His illness seems to have started in Spain at Valladolid where many in his army caught dysentery. It spread so fast through the soldiers that most had a good dose of the runs and many never saw England again. It left Edward so unwell that in the years that followed it sent him many times to his bed, via the bathroom. He was so sick on occasion that his servants mistook him for dead.

Amoebic dysentery is caused by an anaerobic parasite called *Entamoeba histolystica*. Transmission of amoebic dysentery is by the serial parasitic killer's modus operandi, the faecal-oral route.

It is nearly lunchtime and you put down the phone on which you have been pretending to be working. You turn to your PC, remembering to at least print a document before lunch. Do we still print documents? The keyboard does not look dirty, not from a distance anyway, but it was used by someone before you, someone carrying a smear of faeces on their hands. You know the type. You're soon done, and your sandwich is waiting. Dig in. Wait, did you wash your hands? Why would you wash your hands? It wasn't you that had just been in the bathroom. Your fingers grip around the bread, some mayonnaise squeezes out between your fingers. That mayo needs licking off before it gets everything sticky.

Which one made you dash to the bathroom? The keyboard, your sandwich, or the mayonnaise? Fomites are items that pesky bugs cling on to before being passed to new hosts. Transferred to the mouth, swallowed down into the intestinal tract. They can withstand the stomach's defences. The little critters proliferate and attach to the gut wall, causing epithelial layers to become leaky and fluid to flow through. Some are sloughed off and leave the body with the faeces. It's nice you got rid of them, but they have a habit of firing off as aerosol as you flush the toilet. We need to talk about those toothbrushes you keep on the shelf next to the toilet in your bathroom. Feeling queasy? In the case of amoebic dysentery, cysts or eggs are transmitted in this way because *Entamoeba histolytica* is a protozoan.

You can be lucky and get away without suffering any symptoms, just pass them out for others to enjoy. Or you can develop the painful bloody diarrhoea and an amoebic liver abscess. It appears the Black Prince went for the latter option. From each mature cyst he unintentionally ingested, eight trophozoites would come from dividing nuclei. In the large intestine the trophozoites will multiply again, through binary fission. They can invade the intestinal mucosa, the lining of cells that separates the contents of the gut from the rest of the body. From there they can enter the bloodstream and be transmitted to other organs. Or a new cyst is made, and these are expelled in the faeces to be eaten by someone else as they tuck into their own chicken mayo sandwich.

There was at least one contemporary reference to dysentery when it comes to Edward's end. End of life, that is, rather than rear end. He suffered an acute final illness on top of the dropsy or swelling. Edward's health was failing, he was weak and feeble. Anaemia was likely as intestinal haemorrhages meant Edward had been losing blood in his faeces over the years. Swelling is common in chronic amoebic dysentery, but this also suggests he could have had nephrotic disease (a kidney disorder).

Fourteen years before his death, the prince made plans for his funeral and memorial at Canterbury. The tomb remains at the cathedral and can be visited today. Probably best not to touch it before lunch. The Black Prince, Edward of Woodstock, was heir to the throne but died before his father King Edward III. Instead, the Black Prince's son Richard became the next mortal monarch.

Richard II

Died 1400

'*Sirs, will you kill your king?*'
Richard II

In his promising youth, Richard faced up to the revolting peasants and asked them, 'Sirs, will you kill your king?'

Richard's father was Edward of Woodstock, who we now know as the Black Prince. He has since taken on popular iconic status, probably because he died before he could be king, not having his chance to mess things up. Instead, it was his young son, grandson of Edward III, who became the next king of England.

Richard was only ten years old when he was crowned king in 1377. Still in short trousers, he was too young to rule alone, so the formidable John of Gaunt, Richard's uncle, held the position of steward of England and the highest power.

Richard II's reign is remembered chiefly for his dealings with the Peasants' Revolt, as Richard's place within it was pivotal. In the summer of 1381 unrest came to Richard's lands. He was only fourteen years old. Groups of rebels were marauding through the villages, burning land and buildings, attacking the wealthy and powerful. Richard's army could not be sent to meet the rebels; they were away facing the Scots and the French, carrying on the fighting that Richard's predecessors had not finished. 'Death to all lawyers,' chanted the rebels as they marched on London. They were mad at inequality, serfdom and high rents, and post-plague caps on wages. They attacked John of Gaunt's Savoy Palace and the mansions of the city. Whilst many fled the city, Richard stayed put. He rode out to meet the rebels and listened to them. Things took a turn when the rebel leader Wat Tyler came too close to the King. The Lord Mayor struck Tyler and killed him, and the crowd very nearly kicked off. 'Sirs, will you kill your king?' the young monarch shouted.

At such a young age, Richard had demonstrated he was worthy of the crown worn by his grandfather Edward III. The trials and punishments for those involved in the revolt brought the people under Richard's control. We have a good one here, the people of England thought, but nothing good ever lasts.

Richard grew up to be a self-centred young man who had nothing but contempt for those around him. Whenever the King opened his mouth to speak, he offended someone. Many times, the reign of Richard II has been likened to that of his ill-fated great-grandfather Edward II. Richard was even warned of it. They both annoyed the nobles around them, and they both paid for it.

In a scene reminiscent of the accusations laid at the feet of William II and his court, Richard became overly concerned with fashion and extravagance, whilst his kingdom was neglected. There were accusations that Richard's relationship with Richard de Vere was far too close. It is all rather familiar. With groups conspiring against him, Richard became obsessed with his own kingship and destiny, astrology and the occult, and the sainthood of Edward the Confessor. He declared himself independent and tried to rule alone, but Mother Nature, or God, had other ideas for the kingdom.

In 1391 Richard's people faced a terrible harvest. In 1394 another outbreak of plague swept through an already ravaged England. Plague struck the court as it struck everywhere else. Anne of Bohemia, Richard II's wife and queen, may not even have noticed that she had been nibbled by something tiny. The flea, unseen, had hitched a ride on the back of a rat. When that flea pierced her skin, the bacteria *yersinia pestis* spewed forth into her body. Many now believe that the guilty culprits might have been body lice, but the disease-causing bacteria remained the same.

Underneath her warm, cosy skin, the bacteria had food and could reproduce in large numbers. Its only threat was Anne's immune system as her cells tried to fight off the problem infection. The unseen organisms moved through her lymphatic system and came upon her lymph nodes. Pus built up and she developed large, swollen, pus-filled and painful lymph glands known as buboes. Anne of Bohemia, beloved wife of Richard II, was dead. Richard did not take it well.

In a rage he ordered the beloved house in which she had died, Sheen Manor, be pulled down. Sheen was a royal manor on the Surrey side of the River Thames, opposite the parish of

Twickenham and the royal manor of Isleworth on the Middlesex bank. Richard loved the palace but when his wife died there, he cursed the place and had it razed to the ground.

Richard became even more erratic and at his wife's funeral he even became violent, horrifying those around him by beating the Earl of Arundel with a stick for daring to arrive late and then trying to leave early. Arundel had annoyed the King already, being part of a group conspiring against him. Richard later went after the other conspirators, killing three of them whilst others, including his cousin Henry Bolingbroke, son of John of Gaunt, were exiled.

The division between Richard's small group of trusted men and the nobility at large continued to grow. The latter were upset by Richard's mismanagement of the country and the consequent threat of an invasion from France. In late medieval England, the government was the absolute authority of kingship, but society did have a right to hold the ruler to account. Tensions were high.

When, in 1399, John of Gaunt died, Richard denied John's son Henry the lands and titles of his inheritance due to his father's role in the conspiracy. Unsurprisingly Henry Bolingbroke came looking for revenge. It was not long before Richard lost his throne, forced to resign it before the House of Lords rather than face a trial. Henry Bolingbroke, cousin to the deposed king, son of the protector John of Gaunt, became King Henry IV.

Ex-kings, such as Richard, languishing in faraway castles, tend to be a focal point for anyone unhappy with the new regime and thus, for rebellions. Rebellions such as the Epiphany Rising, a plot in Richard's name that sought to remove Bolingbroke and return

Richard. When the rebellion failed, the new king knew Richard just had to go. It was tricky though. Richard was thirty-two years old as the new century of 1400 arrived, and he was quite well. Rumours of Richard's death had spread to the French court even before 14 February of that year. His days were clearly numbered, one way or another.

Popular perception has it that King Richard II was starved to death whilst being held captive at Pontefract Castle. Thomas Walsingham and others wrote that Richard voluntarily starved himself, in protest, which was in keeping with his dramatic nature. Of course this story also put the blame firmly on Richard's shoulders. For others it was far too convenient for Henry Bolingbroke that Richard had killed himself after hearing of the failure of the Epiphany Rising. Some accusations claim that Richard's starvation was not voluntary at all, but was clearly murder, carried out by he that was threatened the most. Keeping Richard alive would have been dangerous, he would always be a threat to Henry's crown.

Shakespeare's story of Richard's death is far more dramatic. It claims the deposed king was chased about the castle by an axe-wielding group of assassins led by a man called Exton. In a heroic fight to the end, Richard snatched an axe and struck down four of the men before he was struck on the head and killed. The story was a popular one. In 1634 you could visit Pontefract Castle and see the marks in the stone pillars supposedly made during the courageous fight, rather like a movie set. Shakespeare clearly thought that a long, tedious starvation wasn't as dramatic as a fight to the death, and would have stagnated his play about the King. It's probably not much fun watching a ten-day-long play about someone not eating.

If Richard was starved to death then he was unique among monarchs. Over the centuries, the modes of a monarch's death matched those of the population as a whole, with trauma and infection giving way to lifestyle-related chronic health problems, but no other king died of not eating enough. Whilst there was always a threat of poison, arrows, daggers, dysentery and falling from horses, monarchs did not have to worry about not having anything to eat. Whether his starvation was voluntary or inflicted by his jailers, we can't know. As with many of the stories told about dying kings, this is a fitting ending for Richard considering he continued his lavish lifestyle while plague and famine dogged his people. Humans need to eat, often. In the first twenty-four hours without food, the body's stores of glycogen are quickly used up. Our bodies don't hold much in the way of glucose stores, some in the liver, some in the muscle and a teaspoon's worth in the blood. Reserves held in the liver and a small amount in the muscles are soon depleted. Once they are gone, without dietary intake of carbohydrate, the body will need to find energy from other stores. If provided on a plate by a friendly jailer, the body will use the fat and protein eaten. If the jailer keeps the plates of food for himself, the energy will have to come from inside Richard. His brain tissue and heart muscle could make use of free fatty acids and ketones as a fuel source, but instead the liver will make glucose by breaking down muscle using amino acids. This is the process of gluconeogenesis.

After a while, Richard will have felt hangry. Hungry and angry, snapping at those about him and being irritable with everything. His mood probably took a sharp downward turn and he felt lethargic as his body tried to conserve energy. He took to his bed, if he had one in his jail cell.

Over a prolonged period, to get the energy it needs, the body resorts to protein catabolism – the breakdown of body parts made of protein like the muscles, fingernails and bones. Eventually even structurally important proteins will be pilfered, and organs will start to fail. The body directs any nutrients available to keeping organs alive over the other functions of building and repair. Richard would have weakened and felt his heart rate increase, along with a severe thirst and painful constipation. His eyes would begin to sink and gloss over. Muscle wasting sets in and the immune system starts to fail. Wounds become slow to heal and there's a poor response to infection. Body temperature drops and Richard would have felt cold and tired. Starved individuals can be either wildly irritable or lethargic and apathetic. In thin, undernourished people the mechanisms that preserve core temperature are impacted. Those cold damp castle walls at Pontefract must have closed in on him.

The time it takes to die from starvation varies depending on many factors – age, health, weight, and supply of water all play a role. For Richard to have died of this neglect quickly, he would also have to be starved of water, which is a different proposition for the body. Hunger-strikers have been known to survive for forty days and more if they have water.

It does seem strange that starvation alone could have killed this previously healthy thirty-three-year-old in such a short time period. Dehydration or even poison might have played a part. The diagnosis of starvation has stuck though and, usefully for his jailors, the blame could be laid just as much at Richard's door with the cry of 'voluntary' as at anyone else's.

Some say Richard was simply smothered and as ever there are also stories of escape, with familiar escapades of a body left behind to unknowingly masquerade as the dead former king. These tales are becoming rather too familiar.

To counteract these rumours, Henry had Richard's body paraded to London and put on display at St Paul's. His face was visible so it could be identified, the rest of his corpse was wrapped and encased in lead, but this did not exactly squash accusations of wrongdoing. Some even went as far as to claim that this was not Richard's body at all, that Richard had escaped. There followed hangings and imprisonments of those claiming that Richard was still alive and living in Scotland, being looked after by the Scottish court. It must have been a touchy subject. One survival story that stuck was of a man who was said to be Richard being looked after at Stirling Castle, as a guest of the Scots. It is hard to imagine, but he was said to be aiding the Scots against the usurper on the throne of England. This man who we shall call 'maybe Richard' died at Stirling Castle in December 1419 and was buried nearby at the Greyfriars Abbey, which stood near where the railway station now stands in the city.

Back in England the remains thought to be the real Richard were initially buried in Hertfordshire. They were later exhumed and moved to Westminster Abbey by Henry V, who felt a bit bad about how his father, Bolingbroke, had treated Richard. The former king was buried beside his wife Anne of Bohemia. Richard had planned for this and had an elaborate tomb built for them both. He got there eventually. Though nobody really believed the axe-battle story, new evidence came to light in 1871, when Richard's tomb at Westminster Abbey was opened 'for cleaning'. Renovations or cleaning was a great excuse, but the Victorians just loved a good nosy coffin raid as much as the Georgians. Inside Richard's tomb they found his nearly 500-year-old bones, fragments of gloves and those wonderful pointy shoes that he liked to wear. They made drawings and took tokens. Sir George Scharf, of the National Portrait Gallery, made some wonderful sketches of the skull and found there to be no evidence of an axe through the head, or anywhere else. So that put to rest the story of the heroic battle of the axes amongst the stone pillars of the castle prison at Pontefract.

Remnants were found recently in a cigarette box dated 1871 and held within long-unopened archive boxes at the National Portrait Gallery. The box contained a fragment of wood, thought to have been part of the coffin, and fragments of leather, thought to be from the gloves and shoes found in the coffin.

Henry Bolingbroke was now free of his cousin and his ineffectual reign, and could rule England in the name of king, as his father was not able to do. When Richard was deposed, Henry promised not to rule the way Richard had, but to be better.

Henry IV

Died 1413

'*Uneasy lies the head that wears the crown.*'
Henry IV, Act III, Scene I

Many have said Henry Bolingbroke spent his reign feeling guilty and depressed over his treatment of the cousin he grew up with. Indeed he deserved to: Henry had promised to do better, but he did not deliver. In part due to his health, his reign did not turn out how he intended. Henry upset a lot of people when he executed the Archbishop of York, Richard Scrope, for his involvement in the Percy rebellion in the north in 1405. Scrope was denied trial by jury, and condemned to death for high treason. Even the Chief Justice Sir William Gascoigne wanted nothing to do with chopping off Scrope's head. This terrible deed appeared to everyone to have upset God. God's wrath brought upon Bolingbroke a skin condition that has been described as offensive, disfiguring and ultimately hugely impactful upon his reign.

In writings of the time in England and across Europe, his affliction was called leprosy, however it is not convincing that this was indeed Hansen's disease, an infection of *Mycobacterium leprae*. The name leprosy was used to describe skin maladies in general, so it is more likely that this was something other than the disease we now know by that name. Henry's rash was specifically described as being white as snow, giving rise to the idea that it could be psoriasis rather than the nerve-damaging leprosy. Psoriasis causes itchy, scaly rashes on the skin with silvery scales, most commonly on the scalp and trunk, and spreading out from the knees and elbows. Skin cells, which are normally replaced in ten to thirty days, are replaced by new growth in just three or four days, creating a build-up of cells. These autoimmune mediated rashes, where the immune system is attacking its own cells, can cycle through flare-ups lasting for weeks or months, cracking or even bleeding. There is often a trigger that sets off this reaction of the immune system's T-cells and causes them to turn on their own skin. Nails can also discolour and become pitted, and there can be a related arthritis. Psoriasis is not contagious and nowadays those who suffer can try symptomatic treatments, but there is no cure. Light therapy, topical vitamin D, methotrexate, cyclosporin and even modern biologics, monoclonal antibodies that directly block specific elements of the immune system, can help. For some today the answer is to be found in the prevention of the inflammatory process associated with metabolic syndrome. For Henry there were lotions, potions, wine and prayer.

What Henry really died of, we don't know. After his death, conspiracy theories spread across fifteenth-century versions of

Twitter and the idea stuck that Henry IV was killed by leprosy as a punishment for his treatment of his cousin Richard and of the archbishop. One chronicler noted that Henry had raised pustules on his face and hands, making this diagnosis stranger still. When Henry fell ill he woke suddenly from his sleep, shouting out in pain that those around him must have burned his face. This is not a likely symptom of either leprosy or psoriasis – or indeed syphilis or yaws, another interpretation that was toyed with.

These diseases present with an initial painful viral-like illness, with long-lasting rashes, seizures and eventual death. This description does fit with the course of Henry's illness, but it goes against the notion that syphilis was first brought to Europe from the New World by Christopher Columbus, 200 years later. Yaws, which was a chronic skin infection with ulcers and papilloma lumps (benign tumours of the skin), was well known. It was caused by the same bacterium species as that of syphilis. Congenital syphilis has even been mooted, acknowledging that Henry's father John of Gaunt had been treated for venereal disease and it was no wonder, considering his notorious promiscuity. Congenital syphilis, with multiple manifestations within the nerves, liver, spleen and bones, can cause blindness and deafness, meningitis and, yes, skin rashes. However, a congenital syphilis would probably have reared its ugly head long before Henry's first illness in 1405, by which time he was nearly forty years old. It seems more likely that the syphilis story was an attempt to smite John of Gaunt. There were plenty of people who wanted to do that.

Skin rashes are often a manifestation of systemic illness, and for Henry, it was not long before other problems arose. He started to suffer from seizure-like episodes, followed by periods of unconsciousness. In his own will he described himself as a sinful wretch. The vague nature of Henry's rashes leaves us scratching our heads as much as he was scratching his. The question is whether his skin disorder and his final illness and seizures were connected or coincidence. Not being a fan of coincidence, I lean towards the former.

Henry suffered several episodes of collapse and recovery. There were times when he could not attend to matters in person, and other times when he rallied. In 1413, whilst visiting the shrine of St Edward the Confessor, Henry collapsed once again and was carried to the abbot's house, where he died in the Jerusalem chamber. Henry had long believed that he would die in Jerusalem, so his prediction had some merit.

Despite the vague nature of Henry IV's biography and the rehashing of these stories with worsening symptoms as the writings travelled across Europe, Clifford Brewer was specific with his analysis and diagnosis for Henry IV. He described 'a uraemic termination of severe chronic exfoliative dermatitis'. So, he believed that Henry's skin condition led to kidney failure, and consequently urea built up in his blood and that induced seizures and death. Uraemic frost is the name given to the white crystal coating that gathers on the skin when urea is not being filtered out of the blood. Ureamic deposits in the skin following renal failure fit the 'white as snow' description.

All sorts of diseases can lead to skin conditions and skin conditions can induce other diseases. Which came first for Henry IV we will never know. Brewer's ideas fit with what we know of Henry's ailments and death. There is not enough evidence to conclusively diagnose the specific illness of Henry IV, though historians and medics alike have good arguments. Whatever it was that killed Henry Bolingbroke, the King's health, or lack of it, impacted his reign, leading to missed opportunities and years of uncertainty.

Henry IV was interred at Canterbury Cathedral, and it would be nice if his body had been undisturbed for the last 600 years, but you and I know that was not going to happen. Once again there was a mystery to solve and a coffin needed opening.

In the 1690s there appeared an interesting manuscript that had been held at Corpus Christi College, Cambridge, and that raised doubts about Henry's whereabouts. The manuscript detailed a different story about the King's burial that had not been heard before. It said that the men conveying Henry's body from London to his chosen resting place at Canterbury had not completed their task fully. As they sailed along the Thames, they were hit by an almighty storm that very nearly destroyed the fleet. In the panic, the King's corpse was thrown into the Thames, somewhere between Barking and Gravesend (it is after all the little details that make stories plausible). The claimant revealed that as soon as they disposed of the body into the river, the storm moved on and all the lives were saved. Surely God did not still have it in for Henry Bolingbroke?

But was the newfound document reliable? Written by Clement Maydestone, an employee of the archbishop whom Henry had executed, the manuscript was even called *A History of the Martyrdom of Richard Scrope, Archbishop of York*. Alarm bells should have been ringing about whether to take this one seriously.

Clement Maydestone claimed to have delivered an empty box to Canterbury. The Georgians wanted to know the truth and there was only one way to find out if Henry's body had made it to his tomb. Shall we open another coffin?

People in the nineteenth century were not generally concerned with the ethics of opening coffins, and Henry IV's tomb was no exception. Four hundred years after Henry Bolingbroke was laid to rest, a group of Georgians, the dean and resident canons of Canterbury, took the lid off the King's elaborate tomb and laid eyes upon his body once again. There was a smaller, lead coffin within the tomb, thought to be the remains of Joan of Navarre, Henry's wife. She was left undisturbed at least. For Henry though, they had a good look.

The gold cloth that had covered the coffin was disintegrated with only little glimpses remaining. Something made of leather also lay there but was not identifiable. They noticed the rough nature of the wooden box they found. It was lodged partly under a marble portion of tomb and they felt sawing open a section would be best. They pulled back the wood to reveal a lead coffin, surrounded by bales of straw. Upon it lay a cross made of twigs that sadly disintegrated as soon as it was picked up. A piece of the lead was cut out, making a window to reveal below the deep-brown leather covering Henry's body. No mention was made of the smell.

'To the astonishment of all present, the face of the deceased king was seen in complete preservation.' Perhaps they were expecting to see evidence of the ravages of leprosy or syphilis. There was not even any obvious discolouration. They saw nothing to suggest any specific disease in the moments before the air got to the flesh and his face disintegrated. They did not remove the lead over the top part of his head, but they did have a prod. The surveyor stated that 'when he introduced his finger, he distinctly felt the orbits of the eyes prominent in their sockets.'

Those prodding fingers showed that the King was not discarded in the river as the Corpus Christi papers described. Somebody who had it in for the deceased monarch had been making up stories. It would not be the last time.

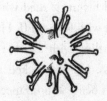

Henry V

Died 1422

'A little touch of Harry in the night.'
Henry V, Act IV, Prologue

Whichever famous face comes to mind when you think of King Henry V, be it Olivier, Branagh or Hiddleston, you will hear the lines from Shakespeare's *Henry V* speeches more often than you might think. In quotes, in adverts, at sporting events.

'Once more unto the breach dear friends'

'We band of brothers'

'Cry God for Harry, England and St George'

William Shakespeare could do notable people very dirty in his historical plays, but Henry V got altogether kindly treatment from the bard.

Henry was the son of the usurper Henry Bolingbroke and spent a fair bit of time in exile, not likely to become king as his father's cousin Richard II was on the throne. Henry grew up fast because he had to. His mother and his uncle died when he was young, and after his father had dealt with Richard II, Hal became heir to the throne. He was left battling with a father who was becoming incapacitated with illness. He even asked Henry IV to step aside at one point, his illness being a hindrance to young Henry's plans.

His father died in 1413, and young Hal is said to have changed as soon as the crown was placed upon his head. Much is made of this change in Henry from rowdy impulsive youth to the next heroic leader, with a belief in his divine right and his dream to reclaim France for England. He may have become more serious once coroneted, but the warrior was in Henry from a young age, fighting in campaigns against the Welsh rebels and Owain Glendower.

As we have seen, stories of death often symbolise how reigns are to be remembered, and tales of impetuous, rebellious youths turned into great men is another common trope used to immortalise a king. Of our many monarchs it was Henry who was cast as another great warrior king, stamping royal authority across the land and taking back France for the crown. He was only thirty-five years old when he died, but he had come close to meeting his maker even earlier, on the battlefield of Shrewsbury in 1403. He was just sixteen years old when he made Harold Godwinson's mistake of looking up at the sky at the worst possible moment. An arrow hit Henry in the face.

Luckily for the young prince it missed his eye but it did go deep through the maxilla, the cheek bone, and it would not be easily dislodged. He broke off the wooden shaft and carried on the fight, but the metal arrowhead remained lodged dangerously close to arteries and nerves. The unenviable task of removing the foreign body after the fight was given to a prisoner turned court surgeon called John Bradmore. He developed an incredible device that went through the wound so he could explore inside Henry's cheek and pull the metal arrowhead out from deep inside the prince's face. He kept the wound clean with honey, making use of its antiseptic, healing properties. He saved the life of the future king and was rewarded handsomely. It is no surprise then that paintings of Henry were made in profile to hide the scar on the side of his face.

In Shakespeare's play *Henry V*, during his speech before the Battle of Agincourt, Henry states that 'he to-day that sheds his blood with me / Shall be my brother', but it was something other than blood that most of them were shedding. Before Agincourt, at the siege of Harfleur, thousands of troops, friends of the King, nobles and lowly soldiers alike contracted dysentery amongst the filth of the military camp. Thousands died of the disease before even facing the French.

It was estimated that Henry had fewer than 10,000 troops left for the battle. The French had as many as 30,000. No wonder that in Shakespeare's play he needed 'A little touch of Harry in the night' to boost morale the night before the battle. Despite such good odds, it did not go well for the French. They rode their cavalry at the English lines where spikes dug into the ground forced them to pull up and the arrows of the longbowmen came down upon them. The English won the day, sticking two fingers up at the French and thus creating endless arguments about the origins of the rude gesture. Henry survived the dysentery that swept through his army and came back to England victorious. He married the French king's daughter, Catherine de Valois, and they had a son, another Henry.

Back in France in 1422, it was King Henry's turn for illness and worse. He had a little touch of dysentery in the night. As we've seen, dysentery has been a large-scale serial killer throughout the centuries. There are a number of enteric pathogens, bowel microbes, that can cause this bloody diarrhoea, including *Salmonella typhi*, shigella and E. coli.

Salmonella typhi causes typhoid fever and has the ability to hang around in the gallbladder of infected travellers, taking it around the world. The bacterium adheres to the epithelial cells that line the gut wall. From there they can penetrate the membranes that surround the cells and get inside. They can also prevent an immune response, invading the very cells that would normally manufacture antibodies to destroy them. The genes that make salmonella so deadly are responsible for most cases of dysentery and can still be fatal today. Complications of a *Salmonella typhi* infection include gastrointestinal haemorrhage, intestinal perforations in the gut and typhoid encephalopathy in the brain.

Typhoid, the disease associated with *Salmonella typhi* (named so as it mimics the disease typhus, which is spread by ticks), can persist in recovered patients for years. Typhoid Mary, now used as a derogatory term for anyone spreading disease, was in fact an Irish immigrant to the US at the beginning of the twentieth century who worked as a cook in and around New York. From her position in the kitchens Mary managed to infect hundreds of people with the disease. She was the first person in America to be identified as being an asymptomatic carrier. Having no symptoms meant silently passing on the disease to those she cooked for. She kept ignoring calls for her to not work, and continued infecting people until, in the end, she was forcibly isolated.

Fifty years later, in the Scottish city of Aberdeen, 400 people were infected with typhoid when a dodgy can of corned beef from Argentina was cut up on a meat slicer in a grocery store. This time though, there were antibiotics to treat the sick. When one small can of meat puts 400 people in hospital even with antibiotics and a greater understanding of microbiology, it is easy to see how the unsanitary, filthy conditions of a fifteenth-century military camp could be so deadly.

Henry V would have felt sluggish as infection from one of these bacteria brought on a fever, abdominal pains and then the tell-tale bloody diarrhoea.

Believe it or not, fever is useful to a sick body. We are always so quick to want to bring a high temperature down with medications, but fevers are part of a defence mechanism developed over millennia. It is not by chance that the body's temperature is raised when it perceives a potential deadly infection. The cells in the human body have an optimum temperature at which they can function most efficiently. Raising the temperature is the body's way of fighting functions that you would rather were not working, like the function of pathogenic bacteria. It makes the host a less desirable place for the pathogen. A rise in temperature is also a signal to other defence mechanisms to act.

When Henry's gut first identified that there was a pathogen

on board, one of his first defence mechanisms would have been to try to expel it, either by vomiting or by diarrhoea. Diarrhoea has two functions. The first is to confuse anyone trying to spell it. The second is slightly more serious. Diarrhoea is the body's way of getting rid of bacteria causing problems within the gut, by emptying out the toxins or poisons fast. For faeces to leave the body in a hurry, you cannot just rely on the action of peristalsis (the normal push–pull contractions of the gut tubes that move food and waste along). If you still need more of a push, then the abdominal muscles will help by contracting. They squeeze as hard as they can to push out the faecal matter fast. That is why it hurts. It can also be worryingly dehydrating as water is pulled into the gut to help dilute and remove the offending bacteria, and in the same instance, electrolyte balance is affected.

Henry V's death was listed as dysentery and that may well have been the primary cause, but there was something else going on underneath with this mortal monarch. It is a similar story to that of the Black Prince: dysentery is rapid and acute. It kills quickly as both King John and Edward I found out. Contrastingly, the Black Prince and Henry had a prolonged illness. Henry was even sick long enough for Catherine to see her husband on his deathbed. She was in England when she got the news, and he was in France. This was not a simple text message followed by a jump on the Eurostar. The journey would have taken some time. Something else must have been happening. Even Henry's physicians decided that this was nothing that they could treat. That seems an unusual stand to take with a disease such as dysentery that, whilst a killer of many, was familiar to the medical men.

More than one description claims instead that Henry had St Fiacre's disease. It is a somewhat vague description, however, because although St Fiacre was the patron saint of venereal disease, he also covered all things colorectal, including haemorrhoids, fistulas and even colon cancers. Incidentally, St Fiacre is also the patron saint of taxicab drivers, box makers, gardeners and people with infertility, but those are probably not relevant to our dying king. In his last, prolonged illness, thirty-five-year-old King Henry wasted away, suggesting something more chronic and sinister going on than mere problematic piles. This suggestion of St Fiacre's disease may mean he had a colorectal cancer.

For fifteenth-century chroniclers and even later writers on the subject, this protracted demise is a problem. If you're going to write positively about a war hero, if you want to immortalise him, then an embarrassing illness associated with his anus makes this challenging. They could not claim that Henry had been heroically slain in battle, but the next best thing would be that other battlefield enemy, infection, like so many others at war. This might explain the differing reports of his death and the prevalence of dysentery among accounts. As we have seen, how the King died is always about more than what really killed him.

Henry V, like Henry I before him, died on the other side of the Channel in France. This time the courtiers wanted to avoid having to deal with the stinking, dripping black juices of king putrefaction as they transported him home to be buried. Leaving his body intact was not a good option. His remains had to be dealt with in some other fashion than just wrapping them in ox skins. Instead, they boiled down the body so the skin, muscles, tendons and ligaments came easily away and just bones were left. They put him in a big vat and cooked him up into a king soup. The bone broth was left in France and his bones were brought back to be interred at Westminster Abbey.

And gentlemen in England now abed, will think themselves accursed they were not here and hold their manhoods cheap whist any speaks, that died with us, of dysentery. I paraphrase the Bard, of course.

Henry VI

Died 1471

Twice king, twice deposed, it was enough to make Henry VI mad. Although Henry was known as Mad Henry, he was not the first ruler to be called mad. Like his grandfather Henry IV, mother Catherine de Valois and his grandfather Charles VI of France, who believed himself made of glass, Henry VI suffered from a mental illness that plagued his reign and left his lands, or what remained of them, in far worse a state than his warrior father Henry V, hero of Agincourt, had left them.

Henry V died suddenly of reported dysentery in 1422 when the young Henry was only nine months old. Power struggles ensued, as an infant could not rule the countries alone (when at aged eight he was crowned king of England, he was also crowned king of France). Henry V had asked his brothers, the dukes Bedford and Gloucester, to take care of his young son in the minority rule, before he was an adult who could make his own decisions. They did so and continuing campaigns against the French were going well. Meanwhile in France a young peasant girl had visions that she must lead the French in battle against the English. Joan of Arc was captured and burned to death for heresy. An enraged France took up arms and was now in the ascendancy. Rivalries ensued in England between those who wanted to continue the fight with France and those who wanted peace. As Henry grew up, he did little to claim his authority, which grew more and more tenuous, and his mental illness became the definition of his reign.

Henry was weak and hopeless, but at least he had a strong wife in the French Margaret of Anjou, who clearly ruled the roost. She could not be seen to be ruling, so she had to do her work in parliamentary affairs via favoured nobles. When a peace treaty with France was announced, unrest followed. The good-for-nothing king was out of his depth and rebels ransacked the streets; Margaret came down heavily on those involved. Henry's right-hand man the Duke of Suffolk could only keep problems at bay for so long. He was executed by rebels in 1450 and riots hit London. Henry fled to Kenilworth, and his cousin Richard, the Duke of York, stepped up. He was heir to the throne as long as Henry had no children. He felt it was his duty to rule on behalf of the ineffectual monarch, and so he fought for the position against Henry's wife. Margaret versus York became the Wars of the Roses (Henry and Margaret were the Lancashire branch of the family. Richard of York, unsurprisingly, the Yorkshire branch), the bloody, ruthless battle for power that lasted for decades.

After learning in 1453 that the crown's assets in France had been lost, Henry fell into a stupor, became insensible and was incapacitated. Whilst he lay in bed, unable to deal with the realm, the fight for power raged around him. Whoever oversees a weak king, oversees England. It was a whole year before Henry came to, reinstated his own men and removed Richard of York. Richard was killed in battle in 1460. The battles raged back and forth, and everyone knew whoever had control of the hapless Henry had control of England. Eventually Henry was deposed on 4 March 1461 by Richard of York's son, who took the throne as Edward IV.

Henry VI and Margaret of Anjou's son, Edward of Westminster, died at the Battle of Tewkesbury in 1471. The grief Henry felt at Edward's death was cited as a possible cause of his own demise. Without his son there to lay claim to the throne, the deposed king was alone and vulnerable. Like Edward II and Richard II before him, the deposed King Henry VI hanging around was a hindrance to the new king. It is believed that Henry was struck on the head whilst at prayer in the Tower.

Ricardians, members of the Richard III Society, will not entertain any idea that Richard of Gloucester, Edward IV's brother, had anything to do with Henry's murder. Of course the Tudors, who had it in for Richard III, were bound to blame him. For years the finger has been pointed at this villainous Yorkist.

The story that Henry died of melancholy after hearing of the death of his son and heir was beneficial to Edward IV, though a bit far-fetched. But after Henry's collapse following the loss of France some years before, it is not entirely impossible to believe. He had a depressive psychosis throughout his life but remained physically fit. Was he stabbed to death? Hit over the head? Or did he merely collapse of a broken heart upon hearing the awful news of his son's death in battle? King Edward, his brother

Richard – and subsequent Ricardians, of course – want us to swallow this side of the story.

It's more likely that Henry was murdered on the orders of King Edward IV on the evening of 21 May 1471. He was forty-nine years old and had been the most ineffective of monarchs. It is claimed today that the King was struck whilst praying in the Wakefield Tower at the Tower of London. It is not known exactly where the King died, so he is commemorated at a spot below a wonderful window made from stained glass fragments from other windows blown out during the Blitz – not a bad place to remember a king that was killed in the Tower.

Blunt force to the head would have cracked his skull, pushing fragments of bone into Henry's brain and splitting blood vessels. A big enough force can knock the jelly-like brain matter into the bony skull on the opposite side, causing further bruising and swelling. Bleeding and swelling would quickly overwhelm the brain. Unconsciousness would follow and the slowing of breathing and autonomic functions, controlled by the brainstem, would soon kill the King.

Despite his faults, Henry deserves our sympathy. He also serves as an excellent case study against hereditary leadership positions. He may not have been an exemplary leader but he was a good and pious man. He did not like fighting and did not take to the leadership position he never chose. A posthumous cult grew around his tragic life, claiming that he had performed numerous miracles, mostly around Hampshire rather than in Yorkshire, strangely. He supposedly brought a dead victim of the plague back to life and he improved many lives, mostly of the weak and unfortunate. Miracles concentrated around a relic, an old hat that Henry had worn to ward off headaches. For the new king Edward IV and his brother Richard III, 'Saint Henry' bolstered the cause of their opponents and any such claims were made illegal. We don't want anyone talking about how good he might have been, thank you very much.

After his death, wax, linens and spices were purchased to embalm his corpse. His embalmed body was initially buried at Chertsey Abbey, but a few years later Richard III had the former king's remains dug up and taken to Windsor, where he was interred near to the man who likely ordered his death, Edward IV.

In 1910 his tomb was opened for a look. Once again they might have claimed it needed cleaning, but we all know what really happened. They found a box containing a jumbled mass of decaying bones in no particular order. The remains of Henry had been moved more than a decade after his death, hence the tangled mess. The bones were wrapped in the rotting remains of the waxy linen material, and there was adipocere, the sludgy result of putrefaction, king slop amongst the decaying bones. One of the party present at the opening of the coffin, W. H. St John Hope, wrote that he saw hair on the skull that was matted with dried blood. Another noted the destruction of the skull as well. It is impossible to say whether these were indeed mortal injuries inflicted on the King, but the conclusion of the time was that King Henry VI had indeed been disposed of violently. Perhaps the same can be said of his successor too. Uneasy lies the head that wears the crown.

Edward IV

Died 1483

Edward of York, also known as the Earl of March, was the son of Richard, Duke of York and Cecily Neville. Richard of York had been killed and his nineteen-year-old, handsome, charismatic son Edward was just what everyone needed. Well, maybe not what Henry VI needed, but he was crowned king none the less.

Edward IV took the throne from his predecessor Henry VI with the help of Warwick the Kingmaker. Warwick was a powerful and influential nobleman on Edward's side (at first). Granted, Henry did not really put up much of a fight personally, but the Lancastrians around him did. Edward was full of energy and appeared strong. It was a marked contrast to the weak Henry VI. Henry's forces were wiped out at the brutal Battle of Towton and the King fled. All was not plain sailing though. Edward made a fool of Warwick when he married Elizabeth Woodville whilst Warwick was trying to broker a wedding deal with France. Later he did the same again, sending Warwick to France to talk about trade, and in the meantime he held games back in England with Burgundians as guests of honour. This was sticking two fingers up at the French by showing he did not need them.

It was not just Warwick that Edward annoyed by marrying Elizabeth and favouring the Woodville family. The nobles were put out by the lowly Woodvilles getting their fingers into all the pies. Both Elizabeth's father and her former husband had fought against Edward at Towton. The senior nobility saw Edward's marriage to Elizabeth as a massive snub. Warwick was so angry he didn't even turn up to the Queen's coronation ceremony. Edward tried to make it up with his old friend with gifts of land and money but Warwick had no need for that sort of thing. He took it, but he had no need for it. What he really wanted was a return of his influence, without the Woodvilles in the way.

Richard Neville, the Earl of Warwick and Kingmaker, went rogue by siding with Margaret of Anjou to bring Henry VI back to the throne. After rebellion attempts in both the north and south, Warwick was killed at the Battle of Barton. At a decisive battle at Tewkesbury, Henry VI's son was killed and Henry VI followed soon after.

Edward brought stability for a while and was able to loosen his belt to accommodate his expanding waistline. He loosened it even further to accommodate the pleasures of the flesh. In the latter part of his reign Edward's court was all vanity and depravity, with the King at the centre of the extravagance. Edward started to use emetics to relieve his stomach of his last meal and make it easier to indulge further. Emetics induce vomiting by either directly tickling the stomach, causing gastric irritation, or by chemically stimulating the chemoreceptor trigger zone within the central nervous system. Once absorbed into the blood, the chemicals will be recognised by the trigger zone and try to rid the body of the dangerous substances through vomiting. Emetics can be dangerous, but it does not seem that they were directly responsible for the death of the King.

The trope of the gluttonous, self-indulgent king rears its head again. With all this indulgence, Edward was not even well enough to fight the Scots, leaving his brother Richard of Gloucester to do the job instead.

Edward IV was only forty-one years old when he died suddenly and unexpectedly. Pneumonia, typhoid and appendicitis have all been blamed and of course any of them could have been a cause. With the carnage that followed Edward's death, nobody was too bothered about recording what exactly killed the King.

When Edward's body was laid out, everyone could see that this was not a violent death. The King's body showed no signs of infectious diseases, such as the pustules of smallpox or the marks of measles or the buboes of plague. Nor was there any wasting of the muscles as one would see with the cachexia of cancer or starvation. Edward did not suffer for a prolonged period, nor was there a massive and sudden event that made him drop dead. So, whilst it is not known exactly what killed the King, sometimes what was *not* seen narrows down the possible diagnosis.

During his short illness Edward complained of chest pain. Nowadays chest pain would suggest heart disease and this is a possibility. Edward's gluttony had led to an increase in weight, which can lead to a metabolic syndrome and an increased risk of coronary heart disease. It was not that common back in 1483, but the extravagant, gluttonous king was a prime candidate. He was after all the grandfather of Henry VIII.

There are other causes of chest pain. Edward had been on a fishing trip at Easter when he became unwell with a cold. It is a possibility that pneumonia killed the King some ten days later on 9 April. Pneumonia is caused by infection in the lungs, most likely by the organisms *Streptococcus pneumoniae*. *Mycoplasma pneumoniae* is also a bacterium that usually infects younger people; Edward was only forty but he had underlying conditions of obesity and related metabolic ill health. Sir Winston Churchill's conclusion in his book *A History of English-Speaking Peoples* was that Edward's death was due to nothing but debauchery.

He would have felt the pain through his chest, maybe in his back when breathing in. There would have been a cough, foul sputum, shortness of breath, and perhaps muscle pain and fever. Percussion on his chest would have elicited a dull sound as the infection-filled air sacks in his lungs had not their usual resonance. Laying an ear upon his chest, his physicians might have heard the crackles as infection got in the way of smooth airflow, causing turbulence. A chest X-ray would have shown white areas where those sacks were filled with the infection.

Of course, the unexplained death of a king led to accusations of murder. There are always accusations of murder when no specific medical diagnosis can be argued for. There was even speculation that Edward drank contaminated wine, a gift from the king of France.

Edward IV was buried in Windsor at St George's Chapel,

which he had rebuilt with his own resting place in mind. There were ten days of ceremonies, and he was laid to rest under a black marble slab. His tomb was surrounded by colourful tributes, jewelled ornaments to celebrate his life. They were later seized during the civil wars of the seventeenth century.

In March 1789 Sir Henry Emlyn was renovating the chapel and Edward's vault was opened. There they found his body, all 6 feet 3 and a half inches of him, laid to rest next to his wife, Elizabeth Woodville. When his coffin was opened, they could see remains of the King's hair and a sludgy gloopy material around his bones. A physician examining the remains took a vial of the sludge. He declared that this was adipocere, the putrefied remains of kingly soft tissue. Relics and hair from his tomb were presented to the Society of Antiquaries in 1790 by the Dean of Windsor, John Douglas.

Another part of Edward's tomb at Windsor was believed to contain the remains of two of Edward's children, who died before him and were the first to be buried in his new chapel. Two-year-old George and fifteen-year-old Mary's remains were in there somewhere, so it was assumed that the children were in the visible offshoot of Edward's tomb. Later when coffins labelled George and Mary were found elsewhere at the chapel, questions were asked about who was buried in the vault next to Edward and Elizabeth. Immediately they guessed that the offshoot of Edward's vault could contain his other sons, the Princes in the Tower whose remains had long been lost. It turned out that nobody had actually looked while Edward's vault was open; nobody actually saw any coffins in there. The whereabouts of the Princes in the Tower remains a mystery.

Edward V

Died 1483 (maybe)

Edward V and his younger brother Richard are missing. Nobody knows what happened to the two sons of Edward IV and Elizabeth Woodville and it has become known as the mystery of the Princes in the Tower. It is one of the most debated episodes of English history and everybody has an opinion. Edward was not crowned, somebody prevented that, but he is recorded as Edward V, King of England. So we are actually talking about the King and the Prince in the Tower, but that's not a phrase that rolls off the tongue as easily.

On 19 May 1483, a few months after the death of his father, twelve-year-old Edward was lodging in the Tower of London. Whilst that makes it sound like he was having a jolly holiday in the nation's capital, he was being held there by the wicked uncle, the one everyone loved to hate, Richard of Gloucester. Another young king was surrounded by those seeking to control him and therefore wield his power. On 16 June he was joined by his younger brother, or rather his younger brother was given up by a mother who had no choice.

In this time of civil war, Richard of Gloucester at first felt that he was doing his brother's work, taking control of the boys now that their father was dead, but he also saw his own opportunity. He took his chance to overthrow them and became King Richard III. By August the boys had disappeared, and it is most likely they were murdered. Richard III had a lot to gain from the deaths of the boys. Thomas More, the Tudor Lord Chancellor, took a keen interest in the matter. He wrote that the boys had been smothered, pointing the blame firmly at the Yorkists, confirming them and Richard III as proper baddies.

As we have seen, usurped kings are a threat. Edward himself knew it. The young king was reported to pray daily in the belief that he was going to be killed, sacrificed. Then the boys vanished. Following Edward's death, Richard of Gloucester declared the children illegitimate and took the crown for himself. Two young boys, especially a king and a prince, do not just disappear. Where are they?

Shakespeare and Sir Thomas More shaped our opinions of these matters for hundreds of years. As they were patronised by the Tudors, we need to take their writings with a cartful of salt. Thomas More even described the specific mode of death of the boys. His story had it that a chap called Tyrrell was asked to deal with the boys, presumably because Tyrrells had a good track record in regicide involvement (see William II). He put Miles Forrest and John Dighton to the task, who 'about midnight came into the chamber and suddenly wrapped them among the clothes. Keeping down by force the feather-bed and pillows hard upon their mouths that within a while they smothered and stifled them and their breaths failing, they gave up to God their innocent souls.'

Humans (even teenage boys) need oxygen. Oxygen is drawn into the lungs with the air of each breath. In the lungs the oxygen passes through the thin cell layer of the alveoli into the blood. In the blood it attaches to the pigment of the red blood cells known as haemoglobin. From there they are given a big shove onwards as they enter and leave the muscular left side of the heart and are pumped through the aorta, the biggest of the blood vessels that begins the arterial circulation. In the right conditions, the oxygen, having found its way to the tissues through the network of blood vessels, will dislodge from the haemoglobin and go about its work. Apologies if you just recoiled from the schooldays' memory of being forced to draw or recite the oxygen dissociation curve. It's OK, you are safe here amongst the murderers and schemers. Smothering the boys would prevent them getting any oxygen into the blood and prevent carbon dioxide from leaving.

Assuming that More was telling the truth, how long would they need to hold the princes down? Well, it's all relative. The brain is particularly sensitive to low oxygen levels in the blood. The perpetrators would have had to hold their nerves long enough for the boys to go through the agonal phase, where muscle spasm, which is induced by an increasing acidity in the blood, would have looked like them fighting back. Their fingers would have started to change to the dusky blue colour of cyanosis. The protest from their bodies, the writhing, would not solely have been a conscious protest but also a physiological one, a primitive need to fight against death as the carbon dioxide levels rise, the heart pounds and the blood pressure increases. It would be no surprise if the perpetrators were hurt themselves; twelve-year-old lads are not always small.

Ultimately the boy's bodies would have had no choice. Without oxygen getting in, the cells would die, attempts to breath would become shallow, the heart would fibrillate and stop, and their bodies would fall back, limp, dead.

Whomever conceived of the plan, or carried out the deed, the Princes in the Tower were killed by someone's ambition. If the boys had died suddenly of an illness, then Richard would surely have said so, showing the bodies to give further legitimacy to his claim to the throne, but he did not.

How and when Edward and Richard died remains a mystery, but there is still plenty to talk about. Underneath some stairs in the Tower, nearly 200 years later in 1674, bones were found. Workmen dug up a box that contained the skeletal remains of two children. They were 'answerable to the ages of the royal youths'. Upon the orders of Charles II, they were interred at the Henry VII Chapel at Westminster and there the bones remain in an urn marked with the names of the missing lads. It is not confirmed these are the remains of the Princes in the Tower, but the location of the bones matched Thomas More's accounts. More had also said that the remains were later removed to another resting place, so it is difficult to take him at his word.

Since Thomas More, much has been written, deliberated and questioned about the fate of the boys. Now we have something powerful in our arsenal that could provide more answers: DNA evidence. There are different types of DNA that might be obtained from the bones. Nuclear DNA could be compared with Uncle Richard (whose DNA we have, his bones having been discovered in 2012). Mitochondrial DNA, which is more likely to be found in the remains, is passed down through female lines and so could be comparable to any descendants of the boys' sisters, should any be traceable, 500 years on.

As we do not know who the bones in Westminster Abbey belong to, do we not owe it to them to find out? The Princes in the Tower were not the only children to have died there in the 700 years to that date. When it comes to DNA evidence, the question is, should we open the urn? Christian burials are performed with the understanding that they will not be disturbed – not that that troubled our nineteenth-century predecessors, who delighted in opening coffin after coffin just to have a look. What has changed? And where should one draw the line? Philippa Langley, the wonderfully determined Ricardian who found Richard of Gloucester under his car-parking spot 700 years after his burial in an abbey, believes we should study the remains in Westminster.

A wonderfully intricate theory by art historian Jack Leslau in the 1990s claimed that the boys survived, grew to adulthood, married and had families of their own. He even named them as Sir Edward Guildford and Dr John Clement, a physician who married More's adoptive daughter and held office as President of the Royal College of Physicians. It was all based around a Holbein painting in which Leslau thought he saw clues about the boys' survival. The painting depicted More's family with the figure of a young man standing at the highest point, normally an important position in such a painting. There were also insignia that Leslau claimed gave clues that the rightful heir was depicted in the painting. He tried to obtain permission to access the remains of Clement and Guildford family members, as well as those of Edward IV. As far as I can tell, that has not yet happened. I doubt it will unless future monarchs or presidents have other thoughts on the matter. Wonderful as it sounds, not all of it adds up. Too many people had it in for Henry VIII and his successors, Catholic and Protestant alike, to keep such a secret, to never use it against the rulers.

This was not the only survival story doing the rounds. In 2021, Ricardians declared that a church in Devon provides us with a treasure trove of clues to suggest that Edward may have lived beyond 1483 and his days as a captive in the Tower. John Evans, the man believed to have been the missing monarch, is buried at the church. His effigy looks up at a stained-glass portrait of Edward, below a crown. A depiction of Evans holding a crown and symbols of royalty can be found there, as well as tell-tale symbols of the House of York.

Without testing there is no way of proving that any of these bodies belonged to the young princes. The Church and the royal family have so far refused any investigation into the interred bones that lie in Westminster Abbey. Even if the bones could be named as young Edward and Richard, they won't be telling us anything about how the boys died or who might have killed them.

Richard III

Died 1485

Richard III was the scoundrel we have spent centuries loving to hate. On 22 August 1485, the modern era began as a blade struck through the helmetless skull of the King, exposing Richard's brains to the blood-soaked battlefield at Bosworth and leaving a king-shaped gap for Henry Tudor to fill.

Richard III was the brother of King Edward IV. They had grown up together in a time of bloody civil war, their father Richard of York being brutally beheaded when Richard Jr was only a child. As the King's brother, he looked after the kingdom's interests in the north where, in Yorkshire particularly, he was highly thought of. Until his brother's unexpected death, Richard was not likely to be putting on any crown. Edward had an heir and a spare, Richard's nephews, the boys Edward and Richard. When Edward IV died, Richard of Gloucester became the protector to Edward's son. For Richard to be king himself, there were two young men in the way, and it was not enough to just declare them illegitimate. As ever, a swarm of eager characters were looking for their own power via control of the child king. Keeping usurped kings alive, as we have seen, is to maintain a threat. Even from behind bars they will have supporters on the outside, using their names to cause trouble.

Sometime in the summer of 1483, the young King Edward and his brother simply disappeared. They were seen playing archery in the grounds of the Tower and then never seen again. Not by anyone willing to tell of it anyway. Wherever they went, they were known for ever as the Princes in the Tower. Ricardians, devotees of Richard III, emphatically believe that Richard did not order the deaths of the boys. They offer up other suspects and claim this terrible accusation was merely Tudor propaganda, a smear campaign to paint Richard as the villain and shine legitimacy on the crown of Henry VII. Ricardians also claim it's impossible for the soldierly Richard to have had a hunchback. Shakespeare's version of Richard III made him out to be a tyrant equipped with a hunch, a withered arm and a murderous vengeful streak.

Until recently Richard's remains were lost. Early sources revealed that he was buried at the Greyfriars Church in the Midlands city of Leicester. They wrote that Richard's body was thrown over the back of a horse and led off towards the city walls. There it was displayed for a day or two and then buried at the church. Another source claimed that he was later dug up and thrown in the river. The same story of kingly remains discarded in a river has been told about William I, William II, Stephen and his wife Matilda, as well as Henry IV.

Before 2012, we knew Richard III died at the Battle of

Bosworth in 1485 and his death was traumatic (meaning that it was caused by physical trauma). Someone will probably suggest poison at any minute (someone usually does), but that Richard III died on the field at Bosworth is not contested.

In 2012, 527 years after his death, Ricardian Philippa Langley led a team to find the king under a council office car park in the city. This was the site of the old Greyfriar's Church where Richard may have been buried. The excavation was closely watched by keen members of the press from around the world. The newspapers were eager to show off the letter R that was spray-painted on the car park. Richard? Rex? Really bonkers project?

Trenches were dug looking for walls or any remains of the church below the modern concrete. What they found was remarkable. Under the top layer were the hastily buried remains of a man. He had been placed in the choir; a spot usually reserved for honoured burials. He had battle wounds consistent with stories of Richard's death and, most surprisingly, he had a marked spinal deformity. This really did look like it could be Richard. What a find.

The University of Leicester researchers laid out the remains and examined them in detail with the help of CT scans. As a surprise to all those who believed that the hunchback label was an erroneous Tudor addition to the story, his spine was curved into a question mark. He had a striking scoliosis, which meant his height was reduced, and one shoulder may have sat higher than the other. He was slight, which was in keeping with contemporary descriptions of his being feminine in stature. The scoliosis would probably have caused him a lot of pain. Shakespeare had written the truth after all, except Richard did not appear to have the withered arm that the Bard gave him.

There was evidence of eleven distinct injuries that had been deep enough to leave marks on bone. Nine of them were to the head and two of those could have been fatal. The most likely fatal blow was to the base of the back of the king's head. He had a large, sharp force trauma to the inferior aspect of the skull. A blade had sliced through the bone, laying bare the brain tissue, slashing through the brainstem that controls the autonomic functions of breathing and heartbeat and through the nervous tissue that ran down his crooked spine. The blade left a mark on the inside of the skull on the opposite side, meaning the metal carved right through the brain. Richard would not have known much about it.

There were further penetrating injuries, by a sharp-edged sword or dagger perhaps. Richard III had been surrounded by Tudor supporters, cut down and hit multiple times in the head, with multiple weapons. He was likely to have been kneeling, leaning forward or in the prone position. There was no horse, even if Shakespeare did say he'd offer his kingdom in exchange for one. He was very unlikely to have been wearing a helmet. Richard's face was not badly touched, unlike many of the remains discovered in a mass grave at the Wars of the Roses battlefield at Towton, which had been shockingly mutilated. It was important to keep his face intact, to confirm that he was indeed dead.

Humiliation wounds were inflicted after death. One had gone through the right buttock and sliced through the pelvis near big vessels. Had this happened before death it might well have been a fatal blow, but this one went in as Richard's dead body was draped unceremoniously over a horse, stripped of armour and clothes to be paraded.

In 2012, whilst the soft tissue had long since decayed away, there was still more information that could be derived from the bones. They showed us that Richard ate game birds and fresh-water fish washed down with wine. As a youngster, before being king, his meals were humbler plates of bread, barley and ale. Radiocarbon dating was used to determine how old the remains were. Measuring the decay of the carbon-14 isotope, with some adjustment for diet, the dating process put the bones between the years 1450 and 1540. Richard died in 1485, in the middle of the range.

Michael Ibsen is the seventeen-generations-removed nephew of Richard III, being a descendant of his sister. Wendy Duldig was another relative through a female line. These two living relatives were critical in the identification process. Ibsen's mitochondrial DNA matched with Duldig's, with the rare haplotype JIc2c being identified. Crucially, the DNA from both also matched the DNA of the bones. Only a small percentage of Europeans carry the haplotype, which helped. The case that the skeletal remains found under the concrete were what was left of the last of the Plan-tagenet monarchs is strong. This was a remarkable discovery and if it had been a film, we would dismiss it as pure fantasy.

If these bones had been found when the Victorians had been digging in the area or when the Georgians liked to open tombs, all that was available to them would have been measuring the height of the deceased and perhaps describing and pencil-drawing the scoliosis and the obvious head injuries. In 2012, bone studies, carbon dating, CT scanning and DNA analysis could not only say that this was indeed the body of Richard III but could also detail some of the injuries inflicted upon him, thus explaining exactly how he died. More than 500 years after the Battle of Bosworth, Richard's story went from, 'maybe he's in Leicester, or lost for ever in a river' to perhaps the most detailed identification and reliable causes of death of all our mortal monarchs.

Richard's remains were interred at Leicester Cathedral in 2015. The ceremony was deliberately designed to honour the reburial of a medieval monarch. The funeral cortège first took Richard's coffin to Bosworth before making its way to the consecrated ground of the cathedral. Thousands came to pay their respects before he was interred in a coffin made by his living relative, cabinetmaker Michael Ibsen. The grave was marked with a modern stone fit for a king. Prayers from his own prayer book were read, just as he had wanted. Better late than never.

Beyond all the Tudor drama, Richard's rehabilitation continues. Perhaps Ricardians can say that *Now is the winter of their discontent, made glorious summer by this son of York*. Considering how he portrayed Richard, I'm not sure they want to be quoting Shakespeare though.

Henry VII

Died 1509

'The captain of all these men of death.'
Attributed to John Bunyan

The first Henry Tudor, the seventh of our Henrys, was a rather disappointingly dull sandwich filling between the massive drama of Richard III and the colossal drama of Henry VIII.

It was not that Henry VII did a terrible job, quite the opposite. He did a good job, just without all the drama. He managed to keep the throne after all, unlike his many predecessors over the previous one hundred years. He made fine work of the finances and put an end to rebellions. He did raise money to go and see off the Scots, but he abandoned that when he angered a few thousand rebels in the south. He quickly put an end to their plans. Henry was right to be paranoid as various pretenders needed to be dealt with, but he remained firmly on his throne.

Henry's father was Edmund Tudor, the son of Catherine de

143

Valois, daughter of the king of France and widow of Henry V. His mother was Margaret Beaufort, the great-granddaughter of John of Gaunt. There was clear royal blood there, but his claim to the throne was a tenuous one, even if he did win it in battle. Growing up in the time of family feuding and civil war, young Henry's fortunes as a Lancastrian were intertwined with the back-and-forth saga of Henry VI versus Edward IV. He was a fit young lad but not a useful military leader to the Lancastrians. Henry fled to Brittany with his uncle Jasper after Lancastrian losses at Tewkesbury in 1471 and he was in exile for fourteen years. Whilst in Brittany, Henry did what young men do, he had fun. He fathered a boy named Roland. Though Roland attended many events at court when his father became king, luckily for the country's stability he did not make any ill-advised claims to the throne.

In 1471, with Henry VI and his son now dead, Henry Tudor became the head of the house of Lancaster. Yorkist Edward IV ruled England. Edward Stafford, 2nd Duke of Buckingham, a one-time supporter of Richard III, had become tired of the King and organised a revolt. Henry Tudor and his mother Margaret Beaufort were now quite useful, with Henry a possible contender to the throne. After Buckingham was executed in 1483, his widow Catherine Woodville married Jasper Tudor, Henry's uncle, who was himself plotting further rebellion. The rebellions failed but in Wales and the Marches, and among those who wanted Edward IV and Edward V back, support for Henry Tudor grew. Henry landed at Milford Haven, gathered support, and marched. At Bosworth in 1485, Richard III was killed and Henry took the crown. Henry had sworn that if he became king, he would marry Elizabeth of York, thus joining the houses together.

So, the reign of the Tudor dynasty began, except it had to be delayed. During Henry's reign a strange disease plagued England. First seen after Bosworth, it spread in an odd manner and affected the wealthy over the poor, the middle-aged rather than young and old, and it preferred the countryside over the crowded cities. It was a fast killer; sufferers could be perfectly well at breakfast and dead by dinner.

Nobody knows what sweating sickness was, what caused it, or how it disappeared so quickly. Nor does anyone know why it seemed to have been isolated to England. It was even known as *Sudor Angelicus*, English Sweat. The first outbreak started in the autumn of 1485, just after Bosworth. Henry of Richmond was due to become Henry VII but had to wait for his coronation as sweating sickness was claiming lives around him. All five outbreaks had ended entirely by 1551. The illness burned itself out, killing a lot of people on the way.

The first symptom was a feeling of apprehension and impending doom. This was followed by shivers, rigors (the uncontrollable shaking of the muscles), giddiness, arthralgia (pain in the joints of the neck, shoulders and limbs). Then the sweating started. The sweating was so bad that clothes and bedding were drenched. It smelled terrible. Palpitations and thirst lasted for a few hours, followed by an exhaustion that just begged for sleep. Close your eyes though and you probably would not be opening them again. Dehydration and exhaustion carried sufferers away, fast.

Sweating sickness was most likely triggered by an infectious organism. Hantavirus pulmonary syndrome is one of the most likely culprits. The viruses are transmitted by biting insects carried around by rats or from their faeces and urine. Hantaviruses do not typically spread from human to human, so it does not fit fully. In big houses, the wealthy lived alongside lots of food supplies and the inevitable accompanying rats and mice. A tentative connection, but it may have accounted for why the illness favoured the rich over the poor.

However, that so many people were in fine health one minute and dead the next, points towards a toxin rather than a living bug. Anthrax perhaps, though anthrax does not necessarily cause a major sweating problem. Ergot was another suspect, also implicated in the dancing plague that swept through Europe in 1518, making people jerk and dance until they dropped down dead. No obvious immunity developed and sufferers could get the disease more than once. There was also such a thing as long sweating sickness, when sufferers who were lucky enough to survive found it difficult to function again for months after infection. We cannot all agree on what the illness was, but one thing we do all agree on is that we do not want to see it again.

When Henry VII himself became unwell in 1497, he isolated young Henry and only allowed a select few to visit him. Henry understood the ideas of contagion from the plague outbreaks of the previous century. This episode is perhaps the origin of Henry VIII's interests in contagion and medicine during his own reign.

As Henry VII's vision started to fail, he became concerned that he would not be able to do the one thing he was good at, the paperwork. 'To bright my eyes' he tried to help his vision with baths of rose water, fennel water, and celandine, a plant of the buttercup family. At the same time, the King started to lose weight and the wasting set in. Wasting was a classic sign of tuberculosis. Until the last century the disease was called consumption as it slowly consumed the bodies of sufferers, wasting them away. He then developed another tell-tale sign, a chronic cough. Progressively the cough became worse, and the King suffered with a tissick – chronic fibroid phthisis or chronic tuberculous infection.

Tuberculosis is caused by the *Mycobacterium tuberculosis* which has had such a hold on humans that it is estimated by some to have caused the deaths of one in seven people who ever lived. This bacterium is over 150 million years old and, despite antibiotics and vaccinations keeping it at bay over the last few decades, it doesn't seem like this one is going anywhere. For Henry VII, the disease was characterised by coughing, blood-stained sputum, and at times fevers, rigors and sweats. Tubercles would have formed throughout his body. These were later described as cheese-like phthisic abscesses by the Scottish pathologist Matthew Baille. They progress from cavities to abscesses in the lungs (empyema) and the same process can be seen in other tissues.

In the early nineteenth century, the inventor of the stethoscope, French physician René Théophile Hyacinthe Laennec, could identify consolidation, pleurisy and pulmonary cavitation in the lungs. He also noted the presence of tubercles and identified that this was the first stage of the phthisis disease. The term 'white plague' was coined in the eighteenth century because of the anaemia and the wasting. For sufferers, all manner of treatments were tried, from fresh air to milk, wolf liver to elephant urine, and even sea voyages to make them sick. Not that one would need the emetic qualities of a sea voyage to bring that lot back up again. Warming drugs of animal fats and butter boiled with honey were given to soothe the wasting patient.

Henry VII was not alone. TB is thought to infect 2 million people worldwide even today. Hippocrates recognised the predilection of the disease for young adults. John Bunyan, author of *The Pilgrim's Progress*, dubbed it 'The Captain of all these men of death', in his work *The Life and Death of Mr Badman*. It has also been called the Robber of Youth and the Graveyard Cough. In Homer's epic poem *The Odyssey*, a description refers to 'grievous consumption' which took the soul from the body and caused a person to 'lie in sickness . . . a long time wasting away.' *Phthisis* is derived from the Greek, meaning 'to waste away'. In 1720 the English physician Benjamin Martin introduced the sanitorium cure with access to open air. In 1882 Robert Koch isolated the tubercle bacillus. Nowadays a diagnosis of TB means taking a cocktail of antibiotics and other medications. With a complex immune response and a chronic progression there is still a need for long-term treatment. Whilst antibiotics and vaccinations have kept many TB infections at bay, multi-drug resistant variants are becoming a difficult proposition.

In 1509, Henry VII was too exhausted to attend the Easter Day service and retired to Richmond Palace. It is most likely that the King died from tuberculosis, as his eldest legitimate son Arthur may have done. It is sometimes suggested that Henry VII's heir died due to the sweating sickness. He was young and wealthy, and it would have fitted the bill, but Arthur suffered from a long-term cough and respiratory issue. It is possible that Arthur had both illnesses. After the long-term tuberculosis infection had weakened his immunity and his lungs, sweating sickness came along and finished him off.

Unlike sweating sickness, which was not seen again after 1551, tuberculosis continued to plague humanity. Scrofula was another clinical manifestation of the disease, which became known as the King's Evil. Since Edward the Confessor, 500 years earlier, it was believed that the disease could be cured by a simple touch from the king, or even the touch of a king's coin. There was a lot of touching going on.

Henry VII was interred at Westminster Abbey in an elaborate tomb. He had restored relative peace and stability to the crown, filled the bank accounts with more money than the Crown had ever seen, and provided continuity in the form of a *nearly* adult heir by handing over the reign to his son, Henry VIII.

Henry VIII

Died 1547

Henry VII died just before his son turned eighteen, but everybody just got on with it as if Henry VIII were an adult. There was much rejoicing at a successful succession. Henry was a handsome, charismatic, fit and well-liked youth. He married his brother's widow Catherine of Aragon to keep strong the alliance formed with Spain, and the future seemed bright indeed.

Henry ruled for thirty-seven years and left us with a lot to unpick. Over those years the well-liked youth became a narcissistic tyrant. His self-importance and lack of empathy saw many lose their heads around him. The marriages, tyranny and remarkable changes in both appearance and character make Henry VIII the most memorable, most written of and most reviled of all the monarchs.

In 1511 Queen Catherine gave birth to a boy, a male heir. Again there was much rejoicing. Sadly the boy died two months later and Catherine never gave birth to another boy. Their only child to live was a daughter, Mary, born in 1516. Henry became twitchy for a male heir, and fell for the lady-in-waiting, Anne Boleyn. With the mild inconvenience of a complete break from the Catholic Church, Henry divorced Catherine and married Anne. Anne gave birth to a girl, Elizabeth, but still no male heir came and when Anne was accused of adultery and treason, Henry ordered her execution. Henry's third wife Jane Seymour did have a son, Edward, who was born in 1537, but Jane died soon after the birth, leaving Henry a widower once again. His marriages to Anne of Cleves, Katherine Howard and Katherine Parr did not produce another child. Henry was left precariously with only one young legitimate heir to his throne.

Through this dramatic journey Henry became angry, depressed and vulnerable. He was not the warrior king like some others before him and he managed to undo all the good that his father had achieved with the country's finances. His mood swings affected all around him and his health deteriorated.

He bought walking sticks complete with whistles so that he might summon help if he fell. He ordered spectacles for his failing eyesight, and he became reliant on a wheelchair and a man-powered stairlift. His weight went up to 28 stones, nearly 400 pounds. Henry's main problem beyond simply his weight and his festering leg wounds, was the often-quoted fact that he had syphilis.

It is convenient to say that syphilis was the cause of Catherine of Aragon's miscarriages, but that glosses over the fact that none of his offspring, be they legitimate or otherwise, had signs of congenital syphilis. Of course Henry VIII did indeed have the male heir he so desperately wanted, his son Edward. Edward died a young man, but he was not syphilitic. Henry's illegitimate son Henry Fitzroy also died a young man, but again gave no evidence of a congenitally acquired spirochaete (the bacterium that causes syphilis) running amok in his cells. Congenital syphilis causes an array of symptoms. There can be bone damage, severe anaemia, hepatosplenomegally (enlargement of the liver and spleen), jaundice, blindness, deafness, meningitis and skin rashes. Babies born to women with untreated syphilis can be stillborn or indeed die from the infection as a newborn. It is hard to imagine some of Henry's children dying in this terrible manner due to syphilitic infection while others were lucky enough to avoid it entirely.

Syphilis is a rather easy answer to all Henry's ills. It is, after all, sometimes still seen as a punishment, maybe even divine retribution, despite being a disease that can be passed through normal human sexual activity. Nevertheless, we like to think of the tyrannical, wife-murdering madman as having a dirty, unwholesome underbelly.

Treponema pallidum, the causative bacterium, was first identified microscopically in 1905, but the disease of syphilis, its initial chancre and later manifestations, were known long before that. The treatment given for syphilis was mercury. Henry was interested in medical matters and treatments, so much so that he would make his own ointments, particularly for his legs, and yet there's no mention of him using mercury for syphilis.

Another argument against Henry VIII having syphilis is that for him to pass it to Catherine of Aragon, he would have had to contract it before he was seventeen years old. That's possible, but it would also mean that he'd likely have shown signs of the disease as a relatively young man. As Henry VIII's body was not a private affair and courtiers knew every inch of it, such signs would have been mentioned. After all, Henry's contemporary Francis I of France had syphilis. It was well gossiped about and was treated with plenty of mercury, something neither Henry nor his wives seem to have been treated with.

A marked change in Henry VIII's personality is often presented as a clear indicator of tertiary syphilis, the effect of the infection on his brain. There are, however, any number of reasons why Henry could have been afflicted mentally. One idea has centred around a jousting accident in which Henry was knocked out. Had he suffered a traumatic brain injury, specifically of the frontal lobe, leaving him angry and disinhibited? Phineas Gage was a nineteenth-century American railroad worker. His traumatic frontal lobe injury gave us remarkable insights into the workings of the brain and what might happen if one injures it. Gage was hit by a tamping iron that shot through his skull and went up through his head, clean out the top. Incredibly he survived but was forever changed in personality. He was left rude, disinhibited and not a nice guy to be around. Sounds familiar.

Not only was Henry knocked unconscious for a couple of hours, but he also sustained wounds to his legs. His wounds festered for over ten years. It was said that the stench from Henry's seeping ulcerated leg wounds was so bad that it filled the nostrils of people three rooms away. Henry and his physicians tried all sorts of lotions and potions. Whilst many today point the finger solely at diabetes, the wounds may have been an osteomyelitis.

Osteomyelitis is a debilitating infection within the bones that can produce tracking fistulae, abscesses that become tunnels leading to the skin and the outside. These channels were his body's way of allowing the drainage of the pus from the wound. Henry had constantly discharging sinuses. If they close over, the collections of pus accumulate and can cause fevers such as those Henry suffered from. These fevers were worrying to Henry's physicians; they could see the dangers of the situation. Even now, a long hospital stay and many weeks of strong intravenous antibiotics are required for such a problem, and so deep is the infection that amputation may be the only solution. Diabetes of course can make any situation worse by impeding the healing of wounds.

In contrast, the gummata, the small swellings that are characteristic of syphilis, are not generally painful. They do not close or heal over as Henry's ulcers did from time to time and they do not cause fevers like Henry's. Seeing Henry's bones would settle the question by confirming syphilis or showing signs of osteomyelitis in the leg.

There has been some discussion over the years about the representation of Henry's nose in various portraits. The degradation of the nose was, for centuries, a sure sign that someone had contracted syphilis. The portraits were, of course, not a 'warts and all' representation like that Cromwell later asked for himself. Instead, they were designed to flatter the sitter. Later portraits of Henry were most likely a memory of his earlier, fitter, youthful, vibrant days. The difference between Henry's portraits and the descriptions of him in his later years being hoisted onto his horse by crane could not be more different. It is hard therefore to take his portraits with anything other than a large pinch of salt (on a giant turkey drumstick).

Henry was referred to as Old Copper Nose, but the nickname had nothing to do with his actual nose or syphilis, but rather the debasing of the coinage during his reign. Cheaper metals were added to the coins, allowing for minting at lower costs. Rubbing of the coins revealed a copper nose in the middle of Henry's likeness and so the name caught on.

It is likely that Henry VIII suffered in later life from the non-communicable chronic diseases that affect so many of us in the twenty-first century: obesity, type 2 diabetes, immobility, maybe the related conditions of gout and high blood pressure. The osteomyelitis in the lower leg bones, perhaps worsened by chronic stagnant venous insufficiency and the effects of diabetes, might have prevented healing. Those studying the later por-traits of Henry have suggested Cushing's syndrome, an endocrine abnormality. Symptoms result from increased levels of the stress hormone cortisol, causing weight gain, a rounding of the face and thinning skin that heals poorly.

Henry survived both smallpox and malaria and yet his reign still became defined by his ill health. His medical history extended to his ability, or inability, to father a baby boy that would live to adulthood. An idea has been mooted that Henry's problems pro-ducing a male heir were genetic. The theory is that he was Kell positive and developed McLeod syndrome. McLeod syndrome is a genetic disorder that starts to cause problems in middle age because of an antigen called Kell, found on the blood cells.

Sufferers can develop peripheral nerve damage, heart disease, anaemia and even personality changes with dementia. McLeod syndrome could explain Henry's behaviour, but there's more. Kell positive blood contains specific antigens that could pass on severe obstetric problems to his wives if they don't have them. A first pregnancy will most likely survive as the damage has not yet been done, but after that the problems begin. Kell negative mothers will produce antibodies that attack any future pregnancies carrying the Kell positive gene, thinking it a foreign invader. Just as ABO and Rh blood groups can trigger an immune reaction, so can Kell. As maternal anti-Kell antibodies go for the foetal red blood cell precursors (the ones that turn into red blood cells), they suppress the production of those red blood cells. Newborns can therefore suffer from severe, life-threatening foetal anaemia.

Named after a Mrs Kelleher, twenty-five Kell antigens have been discovered in different populations with different levels of antibodies. Kell antigens are also found in other organs, including lymphoid, skeletal and cardiac muscle and cells of the nervous system. In modern times, these difficulties can be brought on by the sharing of blood in transfusions, but for a Tudor mother, sensitisation to the Kell antigen would have occurred during previous pregnancies, making them antagonistic to the growth of new life.

Henry VIII had six wives, but he also had three mistresses. From all those liaisons, he had four acknowledged children who survived beyond infancy: two boys and two girls – Mary, Elizabeth, Edward (who became Edward VI) and the illegitimate Fitzroy. Both boys died relatively young, and the girls went on to become icons of English history. There were, however, more pregnancies. They all ended in the heartbreak of miscarriage or stillbirth. But the reproductive patterns of Henry VIII could be just a reflection of the times. Many women lost children before birth or very soon after, and giving birth was dangerous for the mother too.

Three of Henry VIII's surviving children were their mothers' first born – Elizabeth, Henry Fitzroy and Edward. Citing that three of his first-born children survived is a plausible explanation for Kell antigen involvement on the face of it, but only a partial fit as it does not explain the survival of Mary (as a sixth pregnancy). This theory seems to involve a lot of luck and coincidence.

Whatever was occurring genetically, Henry's final illness came in 1547. Thirteen years earlier an act of parliament made it not just illegal, but treason, to talk about the King's death. Speculation was met with execution. We do not therefore have a lot of medical records about Henry's last days. It was not until very near the end that Sir Anthony Denny, Groom of the Stool, plucked up the courage to chat to the King about his imminent demise. He requested that Archbishop Cranmer be called. In the snow and ice of a wintery January, Cranmer took some time to arrive and by the time he did so, Henry was near the end. The King gripped his hand to make a sign that he put his faith in the Lord, and so ended the reign of Britain's most notorious monarch. He died, most likely, of renal failure on a background of obesity and other chronic lifestyle-related conditions.

Henry's body lay in state for a few days and was then transported to Windsor. On the way they noticed that bloody fluid was dripping from the coffin. Dead bodies do have a nasty habit of dripping fluids. The man sent to fix the coffin arrived to witness dogs lapping at the dripping king juices. Like the corpulent William the Conqueror 500 years before, Henry VIII's obese remains were subject to the stories of overwhelming putrefaction as a comment on his worth as king.

The contents of Henry's last will has split opinion. Some say it was tampered with. He had described eight possible succession scenarios and a sixteen-person council to look after his son's rule in his minority. But it did not turn out as he had envisaged. Henry had planned to be buried in a huge lavish tomb complete with a statue of him on horseback. He had stolen a grand tomb that had been made for Cardinal Wolsey, but it was not to be Henry's either. None of his children deemed it important enough to spend money on. Henry ended up staying in his temporary vault at St George's Chapel, Windsor, where he lies still alongside his third wife Jane Seymour, the seventeenth century's Charles I and an infant child of Queen Anne.

He left a nine-year-old boy as a child king, to once again be surrounded by those looking for power.

The Six Wives of Henry VIII

Catherine of Aragon
Died 1536

In December 1535 Catherine of Aragon, first wife of King Henry VIII, removed from court, divorced, dejected and sick, wrote her last will. With it she wrote a letter to the Holy Roman Emperor Charles V, asking that her daughter Mary be protected. She knew that she was near the end. She died the following January; she was fifty years old.

There was no discernible explanation for her death, no obvious contagious disease or trauma. It will come as no surprise that there were accusations of poison directed at the King and his new queen, Anne Boleyn. As the Holy Roman Emperor's imperial ambassador to the court of Henry VIII, Eustace Chapuys was understandably upset at Catherine's treatment and death as she was the aunt of his emperor, Charles V. Chapuys claimed

Gregory di Casale was the alleged assassin, but the accusations were unsubstantiated. In court Henry and Anne celebrated Catherine's death, wearing yellow as a snub to his former queen, rather than wearing the usual black clothes of mourning.

As the embalmer cut into Catherine's cold body, he discovered something very strange. Her heart was discoloured; it had turned black. In a bid to clean it further he cut the heart in two, revealing an unusual black growth within it. Thought now to have been due to a rare cancer of the heart, it was a good metaphor for the heartbreak that Henry VIII inflicted on his first wife. Cancers originating from within the heart are exceptionally rare. Made up mostly of muscle and connective tissue, the cells of the heart turn over a lot slower than other tissue types. Indeed the most common of the rare heart cancers are angiocarcinomas (tumours of the lining of the blood vessels) where there are lots of surface cells that turn over faster. If it was a cancer it may well have metastasised from a growth elsewhere in her body. Most cancers of the heart are, however, benign and the malignant ones tend to have a genetic component. It is accepted that the Queen's cause of death was cancer of the heart.

Catherine was buried at Peterborough Cathedral, not as a queen but as the Dowager Princess of Wales as she was when her first husband Arthur died. They completely ignored the decades she was queen, claiming that her marriage to Henry was invalid. Even at her funeral the bishop accused Catherine during his sermon. He had been appointed by the King; he was not going to say anything else.

Catherine may not have had the send-off that a queen deserves, but there is a celebration of her life held annually at Peterborough where she was buried. Flowers are laid at her grave along with pomegranates, her symbol. The twentieth-century queen consort, Mary of Teck, had the inscription on Catherine's tomb changed, upgrading it to say that Catherine was queen of England. Mary of Teck had herself been engaged to the first-born son and heir of the King, Prince Albert Victor, but when he died unexpectedly during an influenza pandemic she instead married his brother, George, who became king. Queen Catherine of Aragon's incredible story remains crowd-pleasing in historical fiction and popular culture. The first of Henry VIII's wives died without witnessing the carnage that he was to bring to another five marriages.

Anne Boleyn
Died 1536

As Catherine of Aragon was being laid to rest, her replacement Queen Anne Boleyn delivered a stillborn boy and her own world started to crumble. In May 1536, only a few months after Catherine's death, the most alarming event shook London and the world. A queen of England was about to be executed by her husband. Accusations of adultery, incest, conspiracy and sorcery against the King were fabricated by a monarch desperate for a male heir. This was an entirely new scenario; a queen had never been executed before.

Women found guilty of treason faced burning, but Henry kindly granted her a beheading instead. The spectacle of burning the Queen at the stake might have turned many against the King, but it was not unusual for beheadings to go wrong. The later executions of Margaret Pole and Mary, Queen of Scots are evidence of that, but Anne was not going to be facing an axe. In a display orchestrated by the King with a somewhat skewed idea of chivalry, she was to be put to death on Tower Green by a sword-wielding Frenchman. The blade would have slashed through skin, muscle, nerves and the arteries of the neck. It met no resistance as it sliced through the spine and easily cut through the soft tissue on the other side. The Queen's severed head fell to the floor. One or two more beats of the heart would have offered up blood from the ruptured arteries in her neck before spluttering itself into fibrillation and then asystole (she flatlined). It was a fast end for the first executed queen.

Her body was gathered up by her ladies-in-waiting and buried at the Chapel Royal of St Peter ad Vincula at the Tower of London. Her remains were supposedly placed in an arrow chest before being buried. In 1877 Dr Frederick J. Mouat, professor of medicine, examined the remains that were found at the chapel during restoration works. Queen Victoria's permission had been sought to carry out repairs in the church, which had fallen into a state of unsanitary disrepair. Proper foundations were needed and so pavement stones were lifted. Underneath they found remains that they moved to the crypt. When it came to the chancel where the body of Anne Boleyn was thought to be buried, they decided that the bodies should be returned and marked with a label. Bones were removed and examined. They were a female, Dr Frederick said, of around twenty-five to thirty years old, who would have been slender. He also wrote that the skull displayed 'an intellectual forehead'. There was no mention of any sixth finger or hand malformation, something that was thrown at Anne as part of the accusations of witchcraft in justification for her execution.

The bones were soldered into caskets of thick lead and placed inside oak coffins. Plates were attached, engraved with the suspected names, the date of their death and the reinterment date in 1877. They were replaced into the chancel. As ever there are disagreements about the remains, and which bones belong to which beheaded noble. Five hundred years later Henry VIII's second wife, Queen Anne Boleyn, still courts controversy.

Jane Seymour

Died 1537

Henry already had his eyes elsewhere when Anne's head rolled from the scaffold at the Tower of London in 1536. Anne Boleyn went from the joy of coronation to the despair of execution in just three years. Anne of a thousand days gave way to Henry's third wife, Jane Seymour. Jane was another of the ladies-in-waiting at court to become Henry's wife and queen. In October 1537 Jane went a step further and did what Henry had been praying for. She gave birth to a boy, an heir to the Tudor throne.

Jane was gentle and peaceful but was also known to be strict and formal. That Henry had removed the head of her predecessor was something that hung over Jane. She was not going to meddle in his affairs, in case he fancied repeating the feat. His new queen had no coronation as the household were in hiding from the plague that was sweeping through London.

Jane had a difficult labour that lasted for many hours. After the boy was born, she started to ail. Jane died twelve days after Edward's birth and may have retained parts of the placenta that became infected. She may have developed a puerperal fever caught from her birth attendants in the extended labour. She may also have been confined to bed with either of these conditions and then suffered a pulmonary embolism as a consequence. All we can say for sure is that Jane Seymour died from complications of childbirth.

Fever was a well-recognised complication of childbirth long before and up until the Tudor period. Hippocrates and earlier Hindu texts referred to it. The classic symptoms that developed about three days after birth were abdominal pain and distention with nausea and vomiting, accompanied by tachycardia and tachypnoea (a racing heartbeat and rapid breathing). It is now understood that childbed fever, as it was known, is due to a streptococcal infection introduced during the labour. It could well have been the cause of Jane's death just days after giving birth.

There was even talk that Jane had been deliberately sacrificed by surgical removal of the baby, to save his life. These rumours have survived since they first appeared as soon as a month after the birth. The claim that a Caesarean section was performed or that she was somehow killed in the process of removing the child (under Henry's approval) has come and gone in popularity in the 500 years since Edward's birth. The circumstances have been debated for so many years, and scores of historians have dismissed any such ideas, saying they are merely embellished stories of King Henry's cruelty – not that he needed any exaggeration.

Alison Weir researched Jane Seymour's death with the help of physicians. Together they concluded that, for a start, there was no operation to remove the baby. Secondly, they were surprised to see no mention of fever, which would have been an obvious symptom to highlight, in a case of puerperal fever. The contemporary writings suggest that Jane had eaten something bad and developed diarrhoea. Weir made the leap that when Jane moved from the bed to relieve herself, she must have dislodged a deep vein thrombosis and suffered a pulmonary embolism. With a history of iron deficiency anaemia, evidenced by Jane's noticeable pallor and a craving for iron-rich quail, not helped by the bleeding, Weir argued that it was not a Caesarean or puerperal fever that killed Jane Seymour, but probably a combination of food poisoning and blood clots.

It was hundreds of years after Jane's death before a new theory was proposed for childbed fever. Ignaz Semmelweiss was a Hungarian physician practising in Vienna in the nineteenth century who became aware that the doctors moving from cadaver to birthing mother without washing were increasing the occurrence of childbed fever. He realised that simply washing hands might reduce the risk considerably. Semmelweiss was ridiculed by a profession that wouldn't listen to allegations that they might be to blame. Dr Oliver Wendell Holmes of Boston came to the same conclusion as Semmelweiss and he too came up against opposition from other doctors who believed they were gentlemen and as such had clean hands, regardless of whether they washed them or not. As for Semmelweiss, he was beaten and lost his mind in an institution just as germ theory was emerging.

Her duty done, Queen Jane was laid to rest in St George's Chapel, Windsor. Her stepdaughter Mary acted as chief mourner followed by a procession of twenty-nine other mourners, each representing a year of Jane's life. For the first time, Henry wore black and mourned the passing of his queen.

Anne of Cleves
Died 1557

Anne of Cleves was the fourth of Henry VIII's six wives, but she outlived them all. She married him young and was only forty-one years old when she died in 1557.

Anne's very short political marriage to Henry VIII was annulled when Henry decided that he was not going to be able to carry out his kingly duties with a woman he was so unattracted to. Being called 'the Flanders Mare' by her husband would not exactly have been enticing for Anne either. Unlike previous separations for

Henry, this one was amicable, and Anne was granted an income and homes. Importantly for Anne, she left with her head still attached to her shoulders.

Anne lived to see two more women marry Henry, his own death and that of his son Edward, whilst she remained a comfortable noblewoman. To some, Anne of Cleves was the most successful of Henry's wives, yet she has been written off as the least significant. This is perhaps why very little has been written about her death. Her last public appearance was at the coronation of her one-time stepdaughter Mary, but her health was beginning to fail. She was allowed to live her final days at Chelsea Old Manor, dying in the summer of 1557. There are few explanations offered as to her death other than she died of a declining illness, likely cancer like Henry's first wife Catherine of Aragon. A historian somewhere along the line wrote that Anne 'most likely died of cancer' and that is all that one can find in any discourse about the death of a one-time queen of England.

Anne was remembered fondly. She was a generous mistress, and in her will she asked that the Queen Mary and her sister Elizabeth take her servants into their employ in their households. She had been friends with Mary and so the Queen ensured that she was given an appropriate send-off. With a tomb on the south side of the altar, Anne of Cleves is the only one of Henry's wives to have been buried at Westminster Abbey. For once, one of Henry's wives was not in disgrace.

At the Chelsea Old Manor she was embalmed and placed in a coffin to lie under yarns and cloths of gold, embroidered with her coats of arms. Wax tapers were burned day and night as masses were said, and a vigil was kept so that her body was never left alone. An open chariot took Anne from Chelsea to Charing Cross and on to Westminster Abbey, where she lay overnight before mourners attended her funeral the following day.

Katherine Howard
Died 1542

Katherine Howard was young. Born when Catherine of Aragon was still married to Henry VIII, she was even named after the previous queen. Teenage Katherine caught Henry's eye and he moved on to her after the annulment of his marriage to Anne of Cleves. By now Henry had grown obese and was suffering greatly with suppurate stinking leg wounds, yet he still wanted to produce another boy to keep the Tudor line intact.

Katherine had been brought up in a household lacking discipline and education. It appears she was used and abused by the men around her. Growing up she was led astray by the girls and boys around her as well as being preyed upon by her music teacher. Thomas Howard, Duke of Norfolk and Katherine's uncle, brought his young niece to court to serve as lady-in-waiting to Anne of Cleves. He had plans for his future. Forty-nine-year-old Henry showered seventeen-year-old Katherine with gifts and land, and they were soon married. Henry's moods and pain grew worse, and his actions similarly soured.

In 1541 Katherine was involved in secret meetings with a young man named Thomas Culpepper, and the Queen's ladies-in-waiting helped with the secret liaisons. Rumours spread to Archbishop Cranmer; Cranmer took evidence to the King. Both Culpepper and Francis Dereham, a courtier, were accused of treason by having affairs with the Queen, and were sentenced to death. Dereham was hanged, drawn and quartered and Culpepper was beheaded.

Katherine was accused of adultery. Henry refused to see her and sent her to her death. This time there was no Frenchman with a fancy sword, Katherine lost her head to an axe. She was not yet twenty years old. The night before her execution she practised placing her head upon the block. The next day, the Queen's head was lifted and displayed to the crowd, another victim of the reign of Henry VIII.

Katherine Parr

Died 1548

The sixth wife of Henry VIII married a man whose wives had never fared well, but this time it was Henry who died first. Katherine, who was herself twice widowed before marrying Henry, went on to marry Sir Thomas Seymour, brother of her husband's third wife and the new king's uncle. A pregnancy came as a surprise six months later. After two of Henry's wives died of cancer and two wives were executed, a second of his wives now died of likely childbed fever. Katherine Parr died within a few days of her daughter Mary's birth, overwhelmed by infection.

Her body was embalmed, placed in a lead coffin and was buried in St Mary's Chapel, in the grounds of Sudeley Castle. Her funeral is remembered chiefly for being the first Protestant funeral in England, Scotland or Ireland to be held in English, rather than in Latin. The chief mourner was Lady Jane Grey.

After a dramatic life in the Tudor court, Katherine Parr was not allowed to rest in peace. Sudeley Castle fell into ruin during the Civil War a hundred years later, having been used as a base by Charles I and besieged more than once. In the chapel, the graves were sacked, and the monuments ruined. In 1782, local gentleman Joseph Lucas went looking for the lost grave and after a spot of digging in the ruins of the church, he found her lead coffin in once piece. When he opened it he was amazed by his discovery. Katherine's body was incredibly well preserved, skin as white as snow, and moist below several layers of cerecloth. The coffin was reopened repeatedly in the years that followed and souvenirs of hair and cloth were taken.

In 1792 drunken vandals pulled her body out and threw it on a rubbish heap. Lucas had to retrieve her corpse and secretly bury it somewhere else. By 1817 when the local rector decided to rebury the remains, he found that they were reduced to bones encircled by growing ivy.

Edward VI

Died 1553

Henry VIII was at last blessed with the son and heir that he wished for when Edward was born to his third wife Jane Seymour in 1537. She had a prolonged labour and died within a few days of Edward's birth. The young boy survived. Across the land there was rejoicing, feasting and much merriment. Could they even hear each other over the constant joyful clanging of all the church bells? Edward was the future, but not for long.

Though strong and receptive to an education befitting a royal heir at first, by his teens the young prince appeared weakened and not quite the prospect everyone had hoped for. He went down with illness after illness despite his father being precious about his son encountering any risky contagion. Henry knew the importance of isolation when it came to contagious diseases. He insisted that the apartments be scrubbed twice a week and that anyone coming in contact with his son be quarantined first.

Anyone feeling sick had to leave immediately. He did not want to take any risks with his precious heir.

Edward was only nine years old when his father lay in his huge coffin, dogs lapping at his dripping juices, with all the indignity in death of any other mortal. Edward became the new king, but he was too young to really have any impact. England was vulnerable with a tenuous minority rule once again. Others made the decisions for Edward, with Edward Seymour, Duke of Somerset, at the forefront. He was not terribly good at it though and things were not going well across England. In a land being forced into Protestantism and Henry VII's wealth having been spent on war, there was growing unhappiness. Somerset did not last long. He was soon removed as protector and was later executed. Up stepped Dudley, Duke of Northumberland. With all the squabbling for power, the young king's wishes were mostly ignored. Edward felt exploited but could do nothing about it.

Edward grew to be not at all like his father physically, though his portraits portrayed him in the same strong stance, hands on belt, demanding the same reverence. Instead, he was a diminished figure, but at least his attitude lived up to his Tudor blood, as he was noted to be especially grumpy at times.

In the meantime, Northumberland was successfully sorting out some of the problems that Somerset had not managed to deal with. Rebels were put back in their places and it looked like a prosperous future was on the horizon. Until the King became ill again. Despite his father's precautions, Edward caught measles and wrote in his own journal that he also had smallpox. Whilst it was not uncommon to see them both together, or in succession, it is hard to imagine the young lad, weakened by consumption and measles, also surviving the onslaught of the smallpox virus.

Many physicians over the centuries have noted the connection between a dose of measles and the reactivation of latent tuberculosis, or consumption. That appears to have been what happened within Edward. After his brush with a virus, he developed a debilitating and persistent cough. He became exhausted and lost weight. There were blood-tinges in the copious sputum he was constantly coughing up. With the measles' characteristic rash, Edward's immune response was also compromised. There was an increased risk of autoimmune encephalomyelitis and increased susceptibility to secondary infections. The measles virus is known to inhibit the production of the signalling molecule interleukin-12 in vitro, a similar pathway to the HIV infection. So measles may well have weakened Edward's immune cells, allowing his latent TB to have its moment in his body once again.

Edward's hair thinned and fell out. His nails, fingers and toes blackened with gangrene. The young man's decaying body stank, and it kept his attendants away. He developed ulcers, probably pressure sores from lying in his sickbed. Doses of medicines he was given likely only added to the problems of oedema and a bloated, painful ending. Young Edward suffered and died the same long, lingering death of consumption as his grandfather, and maybe his uncle Arthur and his half-brother Henry Fitzroy. He passed away in the arms of a faithful servant, Sir Henry Sidney, in July 1553.

After death his lungs were inspected and he was found to have two large putrefying ulcers within them. The bloated swelling of his abdomen may well have been tuberculous peritonitis, causing ascites, or fluid within the peritoneal cavity. His heart was not commented on, which may have provided commentary on the oedema and the pathophysiology of a tuberculous pericarditis, causing the oedematous legs and 'failing pulse'.

Edward died at just fifteen years old after all the turmoil and havoc wreaked by his father in his quest to provide a male heir. Tumultuous havoc was soon to return once again. Northumberland had seen to it that Edward's successor was none other than his own daughter-in-law, Lady Jane Grey.

Lady Jane Grey

Died 1554

The nine-day queen (for thirteen days).

To many, including the dying Edward VI, the very idea of a female monarch was abhorrent. There had not yet been a queen in her own right and Henry VIII had done his very best to make sure there was not going to be one by trying to father legitimate sons. He did leave a male heir, but Henry did not bank on his only son dying so young.

Edward wrote the 'Device for Succession', his plans for the future, in his own hand, in which he searched for a male heir (a Protestant at that), but one was nowhere to be found. The next eight in line to the throne were all women. The Duke of Northumberland, right-hand man and decision-maker of the King saw his chance. It was not possible for him to get to the throne himself, there was no claim, but his family could come to power if he married his teenage son to the youngster Jane Grey, the granddaughter of Henry VIII's sister, Mary. Crucially she was a Protestant. She would make the perfect puppet, and his own son, with no other claim of his own to the throne, could soon be wearing the crown.

On 6 July the King was not feeling too good. As understatements go, this was a classic. Edward's body had failed him, this was the end. Northumberland took a while to release the rather crucial bit of news as he had to make sure his daughter-in-law was crowned queen first, so Mary could have less time to react. He went to work, but things did not go to plan for Northumberland. Henry's daughter Mary came out of her Catholic hiding place to claim the crown was hers. She was, after all, the daughter of a previous king and oldest half-sister of the recently deceased one.

When Jane was told that she would be queen, she wept. She did not want to be queen, 'It is rightfully Mary's crown' she is supposed to have said. This is the sort of line Mary might have wanted her to say. Jane later told Mary that she wept because she was upset about the death of her cousin, the King.

Jane was taken along the river to the Tower of London, to claim the throne amidst much ceremony. Not everyone was happy about it. People were shocked that Jane's mother was carrying her daughter's train. Well, it was a bit odd. After all, Frances, Jane's mother, had a stronger claim to the throne, still being alive and all, but she was not the one married to Northumberland's son, so that made her less useful to those seeking power. Jane's claim was not accepted. She is portrayed as a young puppet, betrayed by the power-hungry men around her, but Jane was always surrounded by strong women and made a few educated moves herself. She denied her husband kingship, saying he could be a duke, but not the king. In return he threatened her that they would have no children and so she would have no heir.

Jane Grey signed her name as queen and for thirteen days (a little longer than the nine days from which she gets the nickname) she held on to the throne. Mary gathered support and many swapped to her side when they saw she was gaining a foothold. Mary had to take the throne by force – the force of axe, through Jane's neck. Jane was beheaded by Mary. Not actually *by* Mary, that would have been quite the scene, but on the orders of Mary, who seemed to have inherited the vicious streak from her father.

Why wasn't Jane Grey burned at the stake? We know Mary I was capable but Jane was beheaded due to her high status. There were no fancy sword-wielding Frenchmen called in for Lady Grey, she faced the axe. Well, she did not actually *face* the axe, she was blindfolded, and she struggled to find her way, needing help. The fight or flight response must have been kicking in. Her sympathetic nervous system would be firing out catecholamines of adrenaline, noradrenaline and cortisol. They would increase her heart rate, increase her breathing rate and dilate her pupils. Her mouth would be dry for the loss of saliva. With blood directed away from unnecessary actions towards the core and brain, the digestive system would slow. Glucose would flood the system, getting ready to provide the energy that might be needed in the coming moments. Her body was preparing to fight or run away. Jane could do neither though, and with the blow of the axe, the nervous systems that were a moment ago in full action were cut off from each other as Jane's head was removed. Mary was queen.

Mary I

Died 1558

Bloody Mary.

Mary Tudor was the first crowned queen of England. Much of what was said of her and her reign reads like a horror story, just like her most famous portrait, which, frankly, is terrifying. It portrays the woman we have all been taught was a ruthless killer who burned anyone who looked at her in an ever-so-slightly Protestant manner. Mary was thin and rather frail with red hair and a fair complexion like her father. She had light-coloured lips and a low-bridged nose. She had a loud, deep voice and her gaze was penetrating, on account of the severe short-sightedness that she had inherited from Henry VIII. Mary was grumpy and stubborn. She was hard to please and had a quick temper. It is understandable that commenters have looked back at her unsettled youth and used it to justify how that quick temper might taint her reign. Her mother was thrown out of court and Mary was declared illegitimate. She was in and out of favour for years before her father died. It is no surprise that, having been threatened with death or life imprisonment unless she renounced her title and rights, Mary might have been negatively affected.

Like her father and her half-sister Elizabeth, Mary survived smallpox, which she contracted in 1528, but her health problems appear to have started around puberty. She developed pains in her head and abdomen. She became nauseated and vomited regularly and she became depressed. Her menstrual cycle became irregular, a significant problem for a woman who might be queen. Other symptoms were trembling of the heart, fainting and unpleasant worrying dreams. At eighteen, Mary fell ill with an episode of worsening headaches, indigestion and anorexia. Lady Shelton, who was looking after Mary in a rather strained environment, was worried that she was going to be accused of poison. Well, that is no surprise, everyone seems to have been accused of poisoning at one time or another. Nobody wanted to treat Mary for fear of being the last one with her before she died. There was a strong possibility they would lose their own head if they were. Henry VIII sent his personal physician Dr Butts instead. Mary improved but later relapsed. She would have undergone bloodletting, which would not have helped and could have contributed to anaemia. Another sixteenth-century physician diagnosed Mary with what he called strangulation of the womb, brought about by abstinence of intimacy.

Not long after the burial of Jane Seymour, Mary needed a tooth extraction. She developed a fever that caused weakness and palpitations, and she was so sick on one occasion, she was mistaken for dead. Her bouts of fever and melancholy continued. Mary wrote in 1551, 'My health is more unstable than any creature.'

Mary's ill health was known far and wide. It had an impact on her marriage prospects across the nobility of Europe, but when it looked like she might be queen, she suddenly became a fine prospect. Up stepped Philip of Spain and though he was not well liked they married in 1554. On their wedding day at Winchester Cathedral the Venetian ambassador noted that 'she was not of a strong constitution.' Despite this impression, it was not long before Mary declared that she was pregnant. The signs looked good and a delivery day was even announced, but when the time came, there was no child. The doctors decided they must have calculated the dates wrong; the heir would be along soon, they said, but still no baby arrived. Eventually the swelling of Mary's abdomen subsided, and her health started to improve. She had had a phantom pregnancy, a pseudocyesis.

Philip left, returning to the Continent, and Mary sank into a depression, described as a melancholia that would come and go. It was not a happy time. After Philip's return she declared a second pregnancy but when it turned out there was no child again, Philip left. In October of 1558 she was gravely ill. She had to agree to Elizabeth being her successor as, sadly, she had not had a child of her own. News was sent to Philip that this was likely his wife's final illness, and she died on 17 November 1558. Mary appears to have had an obstetric, possibly ovarian condition. The phantom pregnancies were possibly the result of ovarian cysts. This may have developed into an ovarian malignancy that killed the first crowned queen of England before she turned forty-three years old.

Dr V. C. Medvei in 1987 and Dr Milo Keynes in 2000 both theorised that Mary had a pituitary endocrine gland tumour. The pituitary gland is a pivotal gland that sits deep in the brain and controls many functions. A tumour of this gland can have local and systemic consequences. Locally it can press on structures in the brain, leading to visual anomalies and headaches. Systemically it is all about the release of hormones; in this case the tumour could have been a prolactinoma, releasing prolactin. Prolactin is a hormone that can cause the loss of menstrual periods (amenorrhoea), infertility and galactorrhoea (swollen breasts that secrete milk). These tumours can also be responsible for depression. On top of those symptoms, which Mary had, prolactinoma can cause phantom pregnancies. Using Mary's distinctive portrait, Keynes also points out the areas that could indicate the associated endocrine disorder of hypothyroidism – loss of eyebrows and hair, redness of the cheeks and also the headaches, depression and deep voice, could be attributed to this type of tumour.

Interestingly, researchers studying Henry VIII's portraits concluded that he could have had Cushing's disease, brought on by abnormal levels of the hormone ACTH, which also originates from a pituitary gland tumour. Could it be that Henry and Mary shared a genetic disorder? Multiple Endocrine Neoplasia (Type 1) is just such an inherited disorder that causes tumours of the endocrine glands. It is rare and symptoms vary between individuals but can include abdominal pain, anxiety, headaches, changes in vision and Cushing's symptoms, as well as the obstetric symptoms associated with prolactinoma. More simply it could be the result of Familial Isolated Pituitary Ademonas (FIPA). Heterogenous FIPA are inherited pituitary tumours that produce different hormones in the individuals affected. Both Mary and her father could have suffered the same disease.

Mary became known as Bloody Mary for the way she made so many around her suffer, but there is no doubt that from a young age, the first crowned queen of England was suffering herself.

At the time of Mary's death a bout of influenza was spreading. It had killed thousands and it is of course possible that on top of her chronic medical problems, Bloody Mary simply succumbed to the flu. She died at St James's Palace at forty-two years old. Her body lay in state for more than three weeks before she was interred at Westminster Abbey where she lies at rest below her sister Elizabeth, who was next to wear the crown.

Elizabeth I

Died 1603

*The mask of youth
and the legacy of smallpox.*

Elizabeth I, with her porcelain-white face, framed by the brightest of red hair and underlined with lavish bejewelled dresses, competes only with her father for the role of most iconic of monarchs. Even amongst the most eccentric rulers of England, and true to her Tudor and Boleyn blood, Elizabeth's story reads like a soap opera.

Elizabeth was the daughter of Henry VIII and his second wife, Anne Boleyn. Accused of treason and adultery, Anne was executed, her head cut clean off by the swipe of a sword in 1536 when Elizabeth was only three years old. Rumours about Elizabeth's true parentage spread early and even more outrageous gossip and scandalous opinions cling to her to this day. In her popular image though, we see the strong-willed, self-assured, independent queen who was married to an up-and-coming England.

Elizabeth did not grow up expecting to be queen. Her half-brother Edward was Henry VIII's heir, and her older half-sister Mary would follow him. When both Edward and Mary died, Elizabeth became queen at twenty-five years old.

A pivotal moment came four years into her reign, when in October 1562, Queen Elizabeth started to feel under the weather. She would not believe it at first, how could *she* possibly be sick? After a few days of worsening viral symptoms, she allowed a doctor to examine her, and he confirmed that she had the dreaded smallpox. As she became more debilitated, those around her started to feel uneasy. Was the Queen going to make it through this awful illness? It took the lives of so many. Importantly, who on earth would succeed her, and would they be Protestant or Catholic?

The virus did not bother itself with religion. Once the tiny organism latched on to the Queen, a countdown began. There is a one- to two-weeks incubation period before the infection makes itself known. The variola virus would at first make Elizabeth tired, a malaise would sweep over her and bring with it pains in her head, back and joints. A fever would slowly rise within her. At this point the Queen would have been highly contagious. By coughing and sneezing, particles can burst up into the air and be inhaled by those nearby. Her maids and ladies-in-waiting were in the line of fire, seeing to her needs and mopping her brow. Lady Mary Sidney too started to feel the malaise. Perhaps this was simply tiredness from the exertion of looking after the Queen, but the pains and fever pointed to something more sinister. She too had contracted the disease.

It was obvious, of course, once the rash appeared. First small pink bumps show themselves on the mucous membranes that line the mouth and throat. Then the bumps spread onto the arms and legs and trunk and would be excruciating on the palms and soles of the feet. Within a day or two papules appear and as pus develops within them, they become pustules. Both the Queen and her lady-in-waiting Mary Sidney went through this. If the pustules break down, they ooze with the yellowy stinking pus, streaked pink with blood. Anyone coming into contact with this gruesome exudate risks contracting the disease, even via the handling of clothes and bedsheets smeared with the bodily fluids of the afflicted.

Complications can make this terrible affliction even worse. Bacteria can infect the lesions, causing secondary infections. Pneumonia, arthritis and encephalitis can all be consequences of smallpox infection which can spread to multiple organs. An uncontrolled, overwhelming immune response can also lead to death. Three in ten people who contracted smallpox died.

If a sufferer's immune system starts to win the fight, the bleeding pustules crust over and scab. If the body can survive this onslaught and fight off the effects of the virus, the scabs will break free, leaving the tell-tale scars of smallpox. Elizabeth's face, though scarred, was not nearly as bad as that of her lady-in-waiting, who was left severely disfigured.

The effects of this horrific infection are not familiar to us in the twenty-first century. Smallpox is the only human infectious disease to have been completely eradicated. The last known naturally occurring case of the disease was in 1977 in Somalia. A twenty-three-year-old hospital cook called Ali Maow Maalin survived the infection. He prevented further spread by isolating, as he was directed to do by workers of the World Health Organisation carrying out a project to eradicate the disease. A year later Janet Parker, a medical photographer at Birmingham University in England became ill with the disease, and her mother too developed signs after nursing her sick daughter. An investigation revealed that researchers at the Birmingham University microbiology department had been studying samples and Janet likely inhaled some escaped particles. Both survived but the disease was not seen again.

When the virus was declared eradicated in the human population, remaining samples were sent to labs for storage in the US and Russia. There was no longer a need for vaccination and those of us under forty-five years old are unlikely to have been vaccinated for this disease. There still exists concern over its potential use as a biological weapon and it would not be the first time smallpox has been used in this way. British soldiers infected Native Americans in the 1700s by handing out smallpox-infected blankets, which lead to thousands of deaths. Without a fully developed antiviral, we are all vulnerable once again.

Elizabeth I was lucky to survive. Her court's prayers for a rapid recovery were answered. Like many a smallpox survivor though, she was left with the marks to tell the tale. Elizabeth I is remembered for rallying England against the Catholic advances of King

Philip II of Spain, defeating the Spanish Armada, her explorers bringing riches back from new worlds, and as a strong-willed, fiery-tempered queen. Image, however, was everything to her and she would not allow mirrors in her chambers. She would only allow a very tightly controlled likeness to be portrayed in paintings and she destroyed any portraits that she disliked.

Many of us will recognise the distinctive make-up she wore to cover the marks. The make-up Venetian ceruse had been used for centuries but it was Queen Elizabeth who gave us the caricature, the white face laden thick with a mask. The art historian Sir Roy Strong used the phrase 'the mask of youth' to describe how the Queen controlled her image throughout the latter years of her reign. She needed to be seen by her friends and enemies as forever youthful, even as her hair thinned and her teeth became rotten. Remaining youthful meant remaining relevant, and being taken seriously. Interestingly, in popular culture, the image of Elizabeth in thicker and thicker clown-like make-up has become more popular since Strong coined his phrase.

The ceruse used to cover her face, neck and décolletage was made chiefly of lead and vinegar. Even the cleansing products used to remove this damaging make-up were made from toxic mercury. Red pigments containing heavy metals were used on her lips, contrasting with the pure white face paint. Her eyes were lined with black kohl (a powder of lead and antimony) and the pupils dilated with drops of poisonous belladonna. Her eyebrows were plucked until thin and arched, drawing the onlooker's eye to the highest of foreheads. Fashions change but the desire to be fashionable at all costs, certainly does not.

Lead was a versatile component of so many products. It was ground into face powders and rouges, pigments and paints, even used as sweeteners for wines. This malleable product could be made into pewter products for food and drink, and was also used to make coins. It was everywhere and if you painted it on your face, it went everywhere with you.

The French would jokingly refer to lead as 'succession powder' as it was useful for bumping off one's enemies as an invisible and slow-acting poison. When powdered into make-up and slathered onto the skin daily there was nothing invisible about it.

Lead poisoning can bring increasing blood pressure, muscle and joint pain, memory and concentration losses, mood disorders, headache, abdominal pains, anaemia, seizures, miscarriage or still-birth, and reduced sperm count. OK, that last one is not relevant to our queen, despite rumours of her being a man, but it was an issue for many.

In the brain, lead particles block neurotransmitter release and corrupt the formation of the neuro-synapses. Neurotransmitters are the tiny chemicals that move between the nerves, sending messages between the cells. The synapses are the junctions between the nerves that allow for communication, using the chemical signalling of the neurotransmitters. If the release of neurotransmitters is prevented by lead particles, then messages do not get through. Not only can the lead prevent release of the transmitters but it also affects the junctions themselves, altering the gaps between the cells and thus inhibiting signalling further. Lead is a disaster for brains, scrambling their connections.

Lead poisoning and its effect on the brain has been a recognised condition for thousands of years. Long before Tudor women were powder-enhancing their décolletage, lead was cited as the cause of countless problems for elite Romans, its neurotoxic effects causing the strange behaviour of many a roman leader. There was even a word for it, saturnine, used to describe an individual whose temperament had become gloomy, taciturn and cynical as a result of lead poisoning.

For Queen Elizabeth, when the toxic chemicals combined with the moisture in the skin, acids formed that would eat away at the cells of her face. Absorbed into the body through the skin, lead and mercury and other poisons were destroying cells inside. The more she aged, the more she feared becoming irrelevant. She needed evermore layers of the destructive make-up to preserve her mask of youth.

Other problems started to creep in. Her hair fell out and her teeth blackened. Recurrent infections of her parotid glands must have been terribly hard to cope with. The parotid glands sit above the angle of the jaw, in front of the ear canal. They provide saliva to the mouth via the parotid duct. The duct empties onto the inside of the cheek and the saliva lubricates the mouth and provides the enzymes that start to breakdown starches as they are chewed. Bad oral hygiene and dehydration can lead to a stasis of the saliva in the duct and seeding of oral bacteria up into the gland. *Staphylococcus aureus* and anaerobic bacteria are the chief perpetrators. Infected parotid glands can not only be painful, hot, red and swollen, but also suppurative, allowing pus to ooze down through the ducts into the mouth. There were no antibiotics to deal with her foul-smelling problem so Elizabeth would have had a mouthful of pus along with a mouthful of rotting teeth and gums.

The Queen recognised that her body was failing her – 'I know I have the body of a weak and feeble woman, but I have the heart and stomach of a king.'

In 1603 Elizabeth retired to Richmond Palace. Her appetite was shot through and she became emaciated. With news of the deaths of friends and favourites she became depressed and hard to manage. Her ladies-in-waiting spread pillows on the floor around her as she strangely stood for hours on end until exhaustion caused her legs to fail and she fell to the floor. As she stood for hours, she was delirious with the visions of ghosts. The description of an emaciated, cachexic Queen Elizabeth lends itself to the theory of a cancer. Cancer could well have been the outcome of years of poisoning by lead and other chemicals. There was no way of knowing, as Elizabeth did not permit any physical examination by any physician. She did not have a post-mortem either, her ladies would not allow it. Of course, this fuelled the fire of suspicion, providing breathing space for gossip of her possible manhood, or of her having had a child, or conversely that she could not have a child due to an unknown rumoured disease in her abdomen. She died on 24 March 1603, aged sixty-nine.

Her predecessor Mary I had so desperately wanted to have children and continue the bloodline that came from Catherine of Aragon, but Elizabeth was different. She did not conform to the traditional ideas of monarchy and motherhood, whether through choice or not.

There was much rumour and intrigue about her reign, and

chiefly around her reluctance to marry or to provide England with an heir. There was the story of a young man appearing, claiming to be the son of the Queen and Lord Dudley. There was a story of the Bisley Boy, in which a changeling boy was believed to have been placed in the cot when the young princess died. The boy was supposed to have played the role of queen into his sixties. These ideas are encouraged by the dramatic stories of promiscuity, incest and the outrageous lives of many Tudor soap-opera characters. Can Elizabeth I not have simply decided that she would only be married to England? Or do we need to explain her non-conformity by filling in the gaps as we see fit? The more shocking the better.

As for the image of Good Queen Bess, it is ironic that the Queen was so paranoid about being poisoned by her enemies but could have been poisoning herself with her vanity and need to display everlasting youth, all along. With no children and no younger siblings, Elizabeth was the last of the Tudor monarchs, and so started the reign of the Stewarts, with the rather confusingly named James I of England and James VI of Scotland.

Mary, Queen of Scots

Died 1587

Mary, Queen of Scots was born to James V of Scotland and Mary de Guise in 1542. Only a few days later, James was dead. For years the story had it that he died of a broken heart. The James Stewarts that came before him had all died traumatic deaths, but James died because of a battle that he was not even at. Upon hearing that his forces had lost the Battle of Solway Moss to the English, James collapsed, dying a few days later. It is not possible, historians will tell you, to die of a broken heart, it is just a way to dramatise the cold that killed him. As a doctor, however, I can tell you that it is possible to die of a broken heart. Broken heart syndrome is an acute condition also known as Takotsubo cardiomyopathy or sometimes apical ballooning syndrome, reflecting the effect it has on the heart muscle, brought on by the massive onslaught of catecholamines.

As James heard the news of his army's losses, adrenaline, noradrenaline and cortisol hormones would suddenly have been released, flooding into his bloodstream. He may have felt pains in his chest and a shortness of breath. He could have felt the irregular beating of his heart. A traumatic event can weaken the heart muscle, reducing the beating function. This is not the whole story though; James may have been unwell already. He was perhaps not at the battle because an illness kept him away. He may well have caught a badly timed bug, and his broken heart, on top of a weakening illness, could be the explanation for the sudden demise of the king of Scotland.

James died on 14 December 1542 and was buried at Holyrood Abbey with his first wife and his two infant sons, who had been born in 1540 and 1541, and had both died suddenly. A mystery illness carried off both boys on the same day. When he died, James had only one legitimate heir left, six-day-old Mary. The baby became queen of Scotland. Crucial to her claim to the English throne, Mary's grandmother, the wife of James IV, was Margaret Tudor, sister of Henry VIII – and equally crucial to her story, Mary was Catholic.

Mary was sent to France when she was five so that she might marry the Dauphin when they were old enough. He became Francis II of France when his father Henry II died a lingering death of brain infection after a jousting accident. Francis himself died at only sixteen years old when an ear infection spread, likely turning into meningitis. Mary was a widow and the pair had not had an heir. Francis's brother became the next king of France and Mary went home to Scotland. There she married again, this time to a Stewart cousin, Lord Darnley. Together they had a boy, James, but soon after the boy's birth, Darnley was murdered in a bizarre incident. As Mary was away attending a wedding, the house where Darnley stayed was blown up, and though he escaped the explosion he was caught by his murderers while fleeing the blast and was found apparently smothered in the garden. The Earl of Bothwell, James Hepburn, was accused of the assassination. Bothwell then controversially kidnapped and married Mary, becoming her third husband. Protestants rose up against the couple, accusing them of murdering Darnley, and Mary was imprisoned. She was forced to abdicate in favour of her young son James, who was being raised a Protestant.

Mary looked for help from her cousin Elizabeth I, but she was seen as a threat to the English monarch and held captive for eighteen years. Catholics felt Mary was their rightful queen and plots were discovered suggesting Mary was planning to overthrow Elizabeth. Mary's death warrant was signed and in 1586 she faced the executioner's axe. For Mary there was no quick slice of a sword, her execution became legendary for being botched. As she was brought towards her last moments, on a scaffold in the Great Hall of Fotheringhay, she removed her gown to show off undergarments of red Catholic defiance. The axe swung down towards her neck, but it did not make a good cut. Instead it sliced into the back of her head. The executioner wrestled with the axe and pulled out its bloodied blade. He attempted another blow and still Mary's head would not come off, hanging on by a sinew. It took a third chop from the axe to remove Mary's head completely. As the head rolled away the executioner grabbed at it, but merely clutched the wig that she wore, revealing her short grey hair underneath. Reports claimed that Mary's lips kept quivering after her head had been severed, as if she was trying to tell the witnesses something.

Stories of post-decapitation consciousness and the question of how long the consciousness remains after a decapitation did not go away. Experiments were carried out during a time of freely available severed heads during the French Revolution. They were spurred on by reports that the head of Charlotte Corday, who was beheaded for the assassination of Jean-Paul Marat in 1793, appeared flushed and angry when struck by her executioner. The question was still being asked in 1905 when a Dr Beaurieux felt that the severed head of executed criminal Henri Languille responded to him when he shouted at it. Beaurieux was adamant that Languille's gaze fixed on his. If consciousness remained for up to half a minute after removing the head, then it's perhaps not removing the head from the body that is the killer, but removing the body from the head. The drop in blood pressure and blood flow to the brain tissue was the true slayer.

These experiments were not merely done out of interest. They wanted to know whether the guillotine, which replaced the axe and its potential for botched beheading, was indeed the most humane way of ending someone's life. Perhaps not if the head remained aware for as much as thirty seconds after the blade came down.

Whilst the onlookers stared at Mary's severed head with its quivering lips, a ruffling noise made everyone stop. How could Mary's body be moving? Her skirts were rustling. Out from under the robes crawled her little dog, who had stayed with her until the end.

Mary was embalmed and whilst her entrails were buried at Fotheringhay, the rest of her was buried at Peterborough Cathedral. James I/VI later moved his mother's remains to Westminster Abbey where they were spotted in 1867 as the dean was looking for the missing body of her son James.

James I (and VI)

Died 1625

'*The Wisest fool in Christendom.*'
Henry IV of France (maybe?!)

If James VI of Scotland (and I of England) turned up to hospital today the staff would have to wheel his medical notes about on their own trolley, so vast was his list of ailments. That did not stop the conspiracy theorists imagining that James was poisoned, done away with on his sickbed by his old favourite Buckingham, with a little help from his son Charles. It was probably because everyone had it in for Buckingham.

James was born in June of 1566, and his mother Mary, Queen of Scots was soon run out of town. James was also without a father as Lord Darnley had been murdered, and so he became James VI of Scotland at only one year old. In 1603 when Queen Elizabeth died, James VI of Scotland also became James I of England. James and his queen, Anne of Denmark, whom he married when they were fourteen years old, came south to claim the throne. The arrival of the new royal family in England could have been a breath of fresh air after the dour later years of Elizabethan rule. The newly crowned James I though, was eccentric to say the least.

He is not remembered in the history books as being a great king, surrounded as he was by a murdered father, beheaded mother, the mighty Elizabeth I before him and the drama of his son's reign to follow. Instead, he is remembered for his rather harsh treatment of both Catholics and Puritans – and everyone in between, in fact. When James believed that a group of witches were out to get him, he became obsessed with them. The group of men and women were tortured in unspeakable ways into confessing to cursing his ship with a storm on his return journey from Denmark, when bringing back his new wife.

James VI and I is not the most beloved of the monarchs. In truth, it has even been hard to come up with a coherent explanation of this king's death, which is fitting for a monarch described as an incoherent, slobbering pedant who was a lazy alcoholic. Still, at least he was not Catholic, and that seems to have been the important part. Even our annual commemorations of the Gunpowder Plot do not really celebrate that King James was saved from being blown up in 1605. Rather celebrations are geared towards the delight of catching and burning Catholics. One cannot help but think that if a different monarch's life had been saved, we might see more made of it.

As eccentric as he was, James did have a thoughtful head on his shoulders. He was well educated, he wrote, published and philosophised. James wrote about demons, werewolves, vampires and how they should all be persecuted under Christian law. He had the King James version of the Bible written (a legacy that cannot be sniffed at) and he himself wrote an anti-smoking pamphlet as he hated tobacco. He once decided to see if there was any truth in the belief that powdered unicorn horn was an antidote for poison. He tested his ideas on a servant, feeding them poison and then the horn (ground down from a narwhal horn that he had been sold as unicorn). Unsurprisingly, the servant died.

Over the years historians have changed how they look upon James, mostly based on their own or society's opinions of homosexuality. There were many rumours of him spending time with 'favourites' but his public displays of affection with Robert Care, Earl of Somerset, and George Villiers, Duke of Buckingham, in particular, were written about regularly. Political and religious beliefs as well as plain old prejudice cloud a lot of commentaries on James, bearing in mind that accusations of sodomy were commonly used to discredit one's enemies. His sexuality was used as a weapon against him.

James refused to attend funerals as he loathed them. Even when his own son and heir apparent Henry Frederick died, he shunned the funeral and instead sent his twelve-year-old second son Charles, the new Prince of Wales, as chief mourner. He missed out on a naked man jumping about between the mourners claiming to be the ghost of the dead boy. The one funeral James couldn't miss was his own.

That occurred in 1625 after the King died of the old man's friend, pneumonia. It was probably on a background of tuberculosis which left him debilitated for years preceding his death.

He had many problems though, with any one of them possibly contributing to his demise.

As a child, James had a drunken wet nurse who was accused of leaving him unable to walk before he was six years old with her bad milk. He had smallpox and measles and constant bouts of colic and diarrhoea. He had renal colic and often passed calculi (hard stones). He suffered with swelling in his legs, pain and swelling in his wasted feet and had pains in his thighs. He had haemorrhoids which bled regularly, and thin, delicate skin that was often itchy.

When it comes to diagnosing the deaths of the Stewart monarchs in England (apart from Charles I) the waters are muddied by all of the remedies and treatments thrown at them. From the concoctions they were given to the bleeding, cupping, blistering, head-shaving and application of red-hot irons, who knows what they actually died of, maybe even the exuberance of their physicians?

It is possible that James I had consumption. The descriptions of his dishevelled appearance, wasting away with nails blackening and hair falling out, are reminiscent of Edward VI at his end. James also displayed signs of stroke and severely dehydrating diarrhoea. He slobbered, his tongue too large for his mouth, and was incoherent. He had recurrent bouts of fever and convulsions. He had nephritis and arthritis. Sir Theodore de Mayerne noted his enlarged right axillary gland (in the armpit) and olecranon bursitis (in the elbow) and his previously fractured collarbone. It has also been suggested that he became prematurely senile. He developed a tertian ague, a malarial fever, and it looked like this might be the end. Physicians gave him all sorts of lotions and potions, but nothing helped. Buckingham tried to help with a concoction of his own, but the King's health got worse. Hands up if anyone is surprised that he was accused of poisoning James.

With such a considerable medical history and years of obvious decline it does seem farfetched that Buckingham would bother to kill the King. Mind you, one never knows what was in those concoctions. There is of course the possibility that he was killed by medical intervention, unintentionally.

An inspector of his body declared that he had one tiny, shrivelled kidney and another full of stones. His head was 'full of brains and his blood was tainted with melancholy'. A study published in the journal *History of Psychiatry* in 2012 had another look. They inputted the symptoms described into a diagnostic program which gave back some interesting results. Firstly, there was no mention of porphyria, the convenient diagnosis used to justify the madness of his descendent George III. The programme suggested a disease known as Attenuated Lesh-Nyham disease, a rare genetic disorder affecting only males that leads to the accumulation of uric acid. Sufferers have neurological and behavioural abnormalities as well as lots of kidney and bladder stones. The program also suggested Asperger's traits. Perhaps James was not just annoyingly stubborn, cowardly, or uncaring but had a medical condition. With all the ailments and complaints from a young age, it is not a difficult leap to make.

Inigo Jones, who designed the banqueting hall where James entertained and held the ritual of touching the sick against the King's Evil, was given the last task of designing James's hearse and its decorations. Black clothing was handed out to thousands of mourners on the streets, despite the King's hatred of crowds. James was known for shouting and cursing at anyone whose gaze lingered a little too long for his liking. He would not have appreciated his funeral procession.

He was buried after dark, as was the custom, at Westminster Abbey. He was placed in a tomb and almost forgotten. Nobody really knew where he was for a while. The dean had a look in Henry VII's tomb in the 1800s and found an extra coffin in with Henry VII and Elizabeth of York. Their coffins were etched with seventeenth-century graffiti to say John Ware and E. C. had been in there, dated 1645. James was found tucked in with Henry and Elizabeth. Perhaps they got together to compare stories of their deadly consumption.

Charles I

Died 1649

Charles I was the only crowned monarch of England to have been executed. Apologies if that is a spoiler. He lost his head in January of 1649, after the long and costly civil war. The far-reaching arguments over the King's rights, the nation's money and religion were known as the English Civil War. Involving Ireland and Scotland, some refer to it as the Wars of the Three Kingdoms, which sounds like a wonderful Netflix saga. Removal of the King's head led to a period of ten years when England had no monarch.

Charles was the second son of James I of England (James VI of Scotland). His big brother Henry Frederick was the first son and heir apparent, but England did have a habit of losing their first-born heirs. Henry was a popular young man and all looked promising for his future as ruler. He grew up in Scotland and spent most of his time at Stirling Castle. In 1612 he was in London to celebrate the upcoming wedding of his sister Elizabeth, when he fell ill. He died of typhoid in November 1612. He was only eighteen years old.

Typhoid fever is the food poisoning gut infection caused by *Salmonella typhi*. The celebrations in the city were cut short as the prince went down with a fever. His high temperature would have been getting worse by the day. He would have complained of a headache, pains in his joints and crushing fatigue. The pains in his abdomen would have been coupled with ferocious diarrhoea. Doctors tried the Stewart remedies of bleeding, cupping, scarification and shaving of the head, but none of them worked. Stewart corpses must have looked quite a sight.

As Henry was lowered into his grave, a naked man started running between the mourners shouting that he was the ghost of young Prince Henry. Meanwhile, Henry's younger brother Charles, who was acting as chief mourner as his father refused to attend, was starting to feel unwell. Unlike his older brother, Charles survived the illness and went on to become king, a king who would leave quite an impression, though in a very different way to his eccentric father. The problems for Charles had been brewing since the reign of his father. He demanded to be recognised as the divinely appointed ruler by Parliament, who refused to be ruled by one man alone, without the voice of Parliament. Ferocious battles were fought between Charles's supporters and those who wanted more say in ruling matters. It tore the country apart. The parliamentarians came out on top and a captured Charles was put on trial.

He sat upon the crimson-lined chair in Westminster Hall, facing his accusers. The King, wishing to be heard, tapped his cane on the shoulder of John Cook, the chief prosecutor, but the cane's silver head fell off and rolled across the floor. If anyone needed a sign of what was to come, surely that was it. The King was found guilty of treason.

'Whereas Charles Stewart, King of England, is and standeth convicted, attained, and condemned of high treason and other crimes, and sentence was pronounced against him by this court to be put to death by the severing of his head from his body . . .'

As dawn broke on 30 January 1649 Charles made ready for an early-morning death, but he was made to wait. His would-be executioners realised that as soon as the King's detached head was rolling along the floor, supporters of the monarch would proclaim his son Charles as the new king. It was the monarchy that had to be beheaded, not just this one king. Parliament needed to pass a hasty law to remove the monarchy. Eventually, in the afternoon, Charles was taken to the block. He had asked for two shirts to wear as it was a cold January day and he did not want the baying crowd to interpret his shaking as fear. However, shirts can only overcome so much adrenaline-fuelled shaking.

A scaffold awaited outside the elaborate banqueting hall that had been built for his father James. As Charles was walked towards the block, so alien in this familiar place, he noticed it was very low and he asked for it to be raised. They said no. He no longer had any authority around these parts. Richard Brandon was the experienced executioner waiting for the King's neck with his nicely sharpened axe. Brandon knew a low block would mean a cleaner cut. To set the block high risks a messy hack through the face. Brandon did not want to botch the execution of the King. It's worth noting that with covered faces and fake wigs and beards, there is no certainty that Brandon was wielding the axe. With the gravity of killing a king, it is no wonder that we do not know exactly who was behind the mask. That the execution was so cleanly and expertly performed does point the finger at Brandon, who had dispatched other notable royalists and was known to take great pride in his handiwork with the weapon.

At two in the afternoon, Charles lay upon the block, he held out his arms to inform the executioner that he was ready and his head was separated from his body by the swing of the axe. It came off with one clean blow and England was declared a commonwealth. The body was taken away and his head was sewn back on. It was probably not going to make him feel much better, but it was part of the show. There was no visible needlework of course when his vault was opened a couple of centuries later. There was evidence of the axe though. There were tell-tale signs that the head had been cut off the body, with axe marks through the cervical vertebrae.

The fuss around identifying the body of Charles I came about because his remains had not been deposited where they had originally been intended. His corpse, sewn back together, had at first been taken to Windsor but when they arrived it was decided that the space made for him was too shallow. He was put instead into the temporary royal vault that housed Henry VIII and Jane Seymour. They all lie there still, in the same spot today.

In 1813 when the works were being carried out at Windsor, the body was found to be well wrapped in waxed cerecloth. Not much remained on the bones but there was enough to still look like the old paintings of Charles, and he even had the little pointy beard. Happy to have confirmed his identity, they put him back, but not all of him. Sir Henry Halford, Royal Surgeon, took the King's fourth cervical vertebra, the neck bone complete with axe marks, and put it in his pocket to take home as a souvenir. There was no hiding it in a sock drawer; he clearly did not think he had done anything suspect. Instead, he passed the royal neck trinket around at dinner parties and used it as a salt cellar. Later when Queen Victoria heard about Halford's macabre dinner exploits, she insisted that the neck bone be returned to Charles I in his vault at St George's Chapel.

One might argue that with a simple strike of an axe, Charles I got off lightly. Something far worse was waiting for the men who conspired to chop his head off. After the decade of parliamentary rule under Oliver Cromwell, Charles's son, another Charles, came to the throne as Charles II. The restoration of the monarchy in 1660 meant royal retribution. Charles II wasted no time in going after those who had murdered his father. The regicides were hunted down, one by one, and were hanged, drawn and quartered. That was the punishment for treason for hundreds of years. Traitors were hanged by the neck until they were not quite dead. They were then cut down, cut open and disembowelled. Their testicles were sliced away and thrown into a fire. Their entrails were burned before their faces, which can't be that easy considering entrails tend to be wet and wriggly. Their hearts were wrenched from their bodies. Their heads were then cut off with an axe and what was left was cut into four quarters. Limbs were discarded into communal pits and lost for ever, whilst heads were placed on spikes for all to see. Hanging, drawing and quartering was the brainchild of someone with far more than an axe to grind.

Oliver Cromwell, though long since dead, did not escape Charles II's retribution.

Oliver Cromwell

Died 1658 (and again in 1661).

On 30 January 1661, on the twelfth anniversary of the execution of King Charles I, three bodies were hanging in chains on the gallows at Tyburn. All three had long since been dead and buried. Now, on this chilling winter's day, the corpses had been wrestled from their resting places and were hanging on display. The cerecloth-wrapped remains belonged to John Bradshaw, Henry Ireton and the former Lord Protector, Oliver Cromwell. These men were regicides, killers of the King. At sunset the three dead men were all beheaded in a posthumous public execution. Despite Cromwell being long dead, it took eight blows of the axe to remove his head. The remains were discarded, thrown together into common pits. Bradshaw's wife was also exhumed from her grave at the Abbey and thrown into a pit with what was left of her husband. Other parliamentarians who had had the cheek to be buried at the Abbey, built by the kings of old, were dug up and discarded together at St Margaret's, Westminster.

The traitors' severed heads were put upon pikes 20 feet high above Westminster Hall, looking down on the spot where they had put Charles I on trial. The gruesome mummified display remained in place for years, picked at by crows, a grim warning to anyone who might want to take issue with the new king, Charles II. On 5 February diarist Samuel Pepys mentioned that he had seen the heads there, an attraction for tourists as much as a warning against anti-royalist sentiment. The heads of the regicides perched on their pikes through hot summer sun and winter snow until a storm broke the pike on which Cromwell's head had been a rotting ornament. It fell to the ground and supposedly a guard scooped it up and hid it under his coat. He sneaked it home and hid it up his chimney of all places. In the middle of winter, it's hard to imagine anyone hiding anything up their chimney. Our story would have gone up in smoke if anyone had lit a fire below.

Oliver Cromwell became Lord Protector and ruler of the English Commonwealth once he had dispatched King Charles I. He died of kidney complications from malaria and likely sepsis in September of 1658. He declined the treatment of quinine on the grounds that Jesuit's bark, as it was known, was discovered by Catholics. The night that Cromwell died, a huge storm wreaked havoc on England. Change was in the air once again.

Seeing as we are discussing the deaths of the kings and queens of England and Scotland, why dig up Oliver Cromwell? He was not crowned but was king in all but name. He was even offered the title of King but in his purple dressing gown, in one of the many palaces, he decided that he didn't want the title. He enjoyed

214

unrestricted power and in death was treated like the royalty he had fought so hard to bring down. The position of Lord Protector was even passed to his son. His funeral was held at Westminster Abbey and he lay in state at Somerset House. His corpse was embalmed, shrouded and sealed inside a lead case which was then placed in a wooden coffin. None of that feels particularly puritan, but Cromwell no longer had a say. There was a lavish effigy of purple and gold, velvet and ermines for the man who was not king.

There was an elaborate funeral procession through London, based on the funeral of James I. A carriage was pulled through the streets by six feather-plumed horses. Cromwell's actual body had been interred two weeks previously. He had started to smell bad, and his body needed to be disposed of before the elaborate send-off could take place. Nobody wanted to risk another explosive William the Conqueror-like event.

Cromwell's son, Richard, known to many as Tumbledown Dick, wasn't quite the man his father was. He did not hold the power that his father had, and he was forced to give up the position of Lord Protector. The son of the late king was asked to return and restore the monarchy. He became Charles II and sought revenge on those who killed his father.

In January 1661, Cromwell's body had taken some time to exhume. He was interred into the wall of the middle aisle of the Henry VII Lady Chapel at Westminster Abbey. Once out of the wall, he was taken to the Red Lion Inn in Holborn by Serjeant-at-Arms James Norfolk. The pub would not have been for Cromwell's sake, he was far too puritanical for all that. As for Norfolk, he probably could have done with a stiff drink after digging up Cromwell. He also removed a copper-gilt coffin plate that was sold at auction in 2014 fetching £74,500. Bought by an admirer or an enemy? There are scores of people to be found in both camps.

Plenty of enemies would have liked to play football with Oliver Cromwell's head. For three hundred years after the head was stolen, they had the chance. It turned up in 1710 in the possession of a curiosity collector of French-Swiss background called Claudius Du Puy who owned a museum in London. Du Puy claimed that he could sell the head for 60 Guineas. Next it came into the possession of a comic actor by the name of Samuel Russell. He very much enjoyed passing it round at parties. Goldsmith James Cox then acquired the head from Russell in payment of a debt. He sold it to three brothers who thought they might make a considerable profit by displaying it. They were wrong. Nobody was impressed. Interestingly each of those three brothers soon met a sudden death in separate incidents. Now the head was thought to be a curse.

Next, surgeon Josiah Henry Wilkinson put the head on display in all its glory – or gory (or both). Researchers Pearson and Morante studied the head and claimed with 'moral certainty' (which is kind of saying 'maybe') this was Oliver Cromwell's head. Not everyone agreed. 'Fraudulent moonshine', Thomas Carlyle called it. Some have questioned whether it was even Cromwell's body at all on display at Tyburn in 1661. Differing reports as to where Cromwell was buried were probably to avoid any royalist supporters desecrating the grave. The head remained with the

Wilkinson family for three hundred years until, in 1960, it finally made it into a grave again. This time at Sidney Sussex College in Cambridge where Oliver Cromwell had once been a student. The exact location of the burial is kept a secret. Oliver Cromwell may well be remembered as the man who took a king's head, but the story of his own noggin has lasted just as long.

The emptied Cromwell vault at Westminster Abbey was later used as a burial place for the illegitimate descendants of Charles II. Cromwell's body would be turning in his communal grave pit.

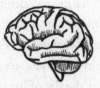

Charles II

Died 1685

'*The Merry Monarch, Scandalous and Poor.*'
A Satire on Charles II by John Willmot,
2nd Earl of Rochester

Born in 1630, Charles II was the son of the beheaded Charles I and his queen Henrietta Maria. With Oliver Cromwell in his grave (for now) and the Lord Protector's son being as good as useless, the monarchy was restored with the fun-loving Charles Stewart, who brought his own brand of jovial amusement. He was notably different to the serious religious figures of Charles I and Oliver Cromwell. It almost feels like Charles II brought colour back to England. After all, Charles did say, 'God will never damn a man for allowing himself a little pleasure.' People liked Prince Charles, and it's no wonder. The young Charles was charming, gracious, self-disciplined and pleasant. He continued to be so, even into his final hours, sitting up on his deathbed and apologising for taking so very long to die.

Charles was eighteen in January 1649 when his father was executed and the monarchy was no longer recognised in England. He sent pleas, begging for the life of his father to be spared, but they fell on deaf ears. Young Charles was pronounced king in Ireland and Scotland but not in England. In Scotland, where he was proclaimed king at Scone, he had to agree to certain terms, chiefly the acknowledgement of Presbyterianism. He went on to gather a following that challenged the new regime but his army was massacred at Worcester and Charles fled. He dressed as a labourer and even did some labouring in disguise. There is not an oak tree in this green and pleasant land that doesn't claim to have hidden the prince. The Royal Oak is one of the most common pub names in England, a hat tip to the tree whose branches Charles clung to in hiding, as Roundhead troops came looking. One thousand pounds was offered as a reward for anyone who gave up the prince. Losing one's head was offered as a punishment for anyone helping him.

After six weeks, he made it to France. Charles was despondent. He had no money and moved around France without much hope. He consoled himself in the brothels, lying back and thinking of England. He remained politically astute, which is just as well because in 1660, England came knocking. Diarist Samuel Pepys wrote of Charles's coronation that he, and many others, drank *a lot*. Pepys partied so much that he woke the next day covered in his own vomit.

We remember the merry monarch for bringing back joy after

years of Puritan ideals, but it was not all parties and excess and merry vomiting. Plague came in 1665, killing tens of thousands of people. Charles fled to Oxford, where he did some more partying. There was war with the Dutch to contend with, and then the Great Fire of London in 1666. Charles and his brother James made sure they were seen to be helping and came out of the terrible situation well. There were still religious tensions between Anglicans and Catholics, and foreign policy issues which had been left unresolved since his father's reign. Underneath the cultural blooming, much of the good that Charles was doing was being paid for through his associations with France and Louis XIV.

Catholicism was worrying a lot of people. James, the Duke of York, was openly wandering around as a Catholic. To the annoyance of many, he was heir to throne. Charles and his wife Catherine of Braganza had no legitimate children, but he had so many illegitimate children with his string of dominating mistresses that he could not count them without invoking toes, but that did not help with succession concerns. Parliamentarians tried to block any succession involving James. Charles stopped them. In the 1670s the fictional Popish Plot was fabricated by a man called Titus Oates. He claimed that there was a Catholic plot to kill the King. Lots of people lost their lives because of it, but still James remained heir.

Charles's parties and mistresses took their toll and led to illness in 1685. He had a painful ulcer on his leg, but that may well have been secondary to that most painful of diseases, gout. This was all the result of a lifetime of excess. A sore on his heel prevented his beloved walks with his spaniels. Instead, one day in January he rode in his carriage, then retired to bed but did not sleep well. Early the next morning, he went about his morning ablutions but when he stumbled out from the chamber he looked ghastly and pale. As his barber made ready to shave him, the King fell into a violent and frightening fit, letting out a 'dreadful shriek'. It took Sir Edmund King a moment before he acted. It was not permitted to bleed the King without the consent of the chief ministers, on penalty of death. But with the King fitting so violently, it was decided that this was an emergency, and so they set about with their lancet. He took a pint of blood from the King's veins, the first of many. Charles's jaw was forced apart to prevent him from biting his tongue during the fit. We would not want him bleeding from the wrong place, would we?

At that time it was thought that the body was made of four humours: blood, phlegm, black bile and yellow bile. Linked to the seasons, personality types and the stars, when the balance was off, the body became diseased. Created in ancient Greece and developed by Roman physician Galen, the theory was that imbalances could be put right by applying an opposite remedy. Charles's treatment was all designed to balance the humours that must have been off kilter, causing such grave illness.

They administered remedies designed to induce sneezing. They applied plasters of noxious substances to the soles of his feet. They cupped and scarified him, applied hot irons to his skin and gave him many different experimental concoctions. His physicians used canthanides, which were chemicals derived from crushed beetles that induced blistering. Blister beetles excrete an odourless, colourless fatty secretion that is an irritant and potent vesicant (causes blisters) and which they rubbed into the skin of the apoplectic, dying King. Traditionally used as a sexual stimulant in livestock, canthanides are fed to the cattle and they irritate the urinary tract when they are urinated out. Canthanides can in larger doses be poisonous to humans. To be fair, poisoning is usually only seen in self-experimentation gone awry. Do not try this at home, priapism is not fun.

The body of the King must have looked monstrous, but the army of top physicians tried everything that they could think of. There were eight eye-witness accounts from beside Charles II's deathbed, among them Sir Charles Scarburgh and the physician James Welwood, who later attended to Mary II. She requested that he write his memoirs for her eyes only. The manuscript was found by her bed when she died and her husband, King William III, had them published in 1699. Welwood's suggestion that Charles was poisoned were dismissed as 'tittle-tattle and grotesque' by Raymond Crawford in his 1910 book, *The Last Days of Charles II*. He pointed out that Charles himself did not even believe he was poisoned. There was the possibility of accidental exposure to a poison, mercury perhaps from the science lab that Charles kept in his basement, but nobody could say that it was deliberate.

Charles asked to be sat up so that he might see one more dawn. He was read the Catholic last rites, marking his deathbed conversion, and died on 6 February 1685.

Henry Halford, president of the Royal College of Physicians from 1820, attributed the death of Charles II to a sudden onset of apoplexy or stroke, and that idea has stuck, but this was not the

King's first fit. Correspondence between courtiers and Charles's brother James was evidence of that. Halford argued that the effigy of Charles II at Westminster Abbey displayed obvious signs of one-sided facial paralysis, clearly from a stroke. Facial paralysis isolated from limb paralysis is rare and the King's speech was not affected. Once again, there is no easy answer.

Physicians and surgeons were by the time of Charles's death performing post-mortems out of interest in the body and not just for removal of organs while embalming. The post-mortem findings were reported by Charles's physician Sir Charles Scarburgh. On the surface of the brain the veins and arteries were unduly full, he wrote. The cerebral ventricles, the cavities within the brain, were filled with a kind of serous matter, as was the substance of the brain itself. On the right side of the lungs, the pleura, the linings of the lung, were firmly adhered to the chest wall. The lungs were also full of blood. The heart was large and firm but displayed no abnormality. The liver was 'livid in colour', engorged with blood, as were the kidneys.

Although many of Charles II's subjects were upset by his death, the Stewarts were not bothered about lavish posthumous remembrance. His last-minute conversion to Catholicism may have contributed to the decision. But they wanted to outshine Oliver Cromwell's procession and awarded Charles's funeral fund £70,000, as opposed to the Protector's £60,000. Charles was interred near his grandfather in a vault beneath the Henry VII chapel in Westminster Abbey. With his death, the crown passed to his brother James. More succession troubles lay ahead.

James II

Died 1701

While we challenged the theory that Henry VIII had syphilis, there is a possibility that at least one monarch did die from the ravages of the disease. James II was the younger brother of Charles II, restored to his position as Duke of York in 1660 along with the restoration of the monarchy. Before that he had merely been the younger brother of an exiled king and put himself to use by fighting, first for the French army and then the Spanish. He came back to England with his brother and was himself crowned king when his brother died in 1685. James was in his fifties by the time it was his turn to wear the crown.

Scaffolding was erected at Westminster Abbey for James's coronation. When it was being removed a part collapsed onto the tomb of Edward the Confessor, leaving a hole in the old lid. Choirman and antiquarian Henry Keepe put his arm in and grabbed something from under the Confessor's bony shoulder blade. He pulled out an ornate gold crucifix. The treasure was presented to the new king, who of course accepted it and commissioned a new coffin for the 600-year-old remains.

James is not remembered with the same reverence as Edward the Confessor. His reign was marred by religious tensions. James was Catholic and tolerant, but the country did not want to be either of those things. He had Anglican children with his first wife Anne Hyde, boys and girls, but only their daughters Mary and Anne survived. When a son, James, was born to his second wife, Mary of Moderna, in 1688, a Catholic succession crisis was on the cards. Protestants wanted James's eldest daughter Mary and her husband William of Orange to claim the throne and protect Protestantism in England. James II was run out of town in the Glorious Revolution of 1688. It was also known as the Bloodless Revolution as there was no fighting. James was deposed and sent into exile in France. He made up for the lack of spilled blood with a wonderful display of unstoppable nosebleeds. They might have been a sign of something sinister going on inside his body.

With all the brothel visits and multiple mistresses, it comes as no surprise that James might have contracted syphilis. Syphilis was widespread and most of the medical advertisements in the newspapers and pamphlets of 1660–1715 held in the records of the British Library refer to venereal disease. It was a condition well known to the Stewarts, though they did not know the causative agent, *Treponema pallidum*, a spirochaete bacterium.

First signs of the disease are painless ulcers or chancres, followed by blotchy red rashes and flu-like symptoms. The initial stages are followed by a latent period. Years can go by without any symptoms, whilst the bacteria sit there, waiting to cause damage. Syphilis can cause irreversible damage to skin, bones, organs and nerves. So too can mercury, the very treatment used for syphilis. A Dr Frazier, who was known for treating James's big brother Charles for the disease, may well have looked after James also. Mercury was administered in all sorts of inventive ways. It could be rubbed on the skin, placed in plasters applied to the skin, taken by mouth as tablets or tonics, or given by intramuscular injection. The fumigation method applied mercury steam all over the body or directly to the genitals, and then there was the urethral syringe. A big needle up the urethra gives a direct route to the supposed cause – why not?

One aim of mercury treatment was salivation. Saliva leaving the body was thought to balance the humours which had been affected by the disease. Mercury's action inhibits the degradation of the catecholamines like adrenaline, and so salivation, sweating, heart rate, blood pressure all get out of hand. As the public health messages would warn, two minutes with Venus, two years with mercury. 'Then fall apart and die' probably took up too much space for the poster.

In later life, away from any thoughts of the crown, James's days were filled with prayer, observing fasts and penance. He wore a sharp studded chain that acted like a cilice, digging into his flesh as a means of repentance. He prayed a lot. In the late summer of 1701 James was attending Mass when he suffered a stroke. It did not kill him but left him with a lingering right-sided hemiplegia (a paralysis of the limbs on one side of the body). The first was followed by further attacks, each leaving him more debilitated. He vomited a large volume of blood, which has been put down to a bleed from a syphilitic aneurysm. It could be that the stroke was a result of the vascular damage done by syphilis bacterium within his brain. Meningovascular syphilis is one form of neuro-syphilis or tertiary syphilis. The bacteria destroy the blood vessels supplying the brain tissue. After one last visit from old friend Louis XIV, James died on 16 September 1701.

What happened to James's body was not a simple burial. Not at first anyway. His heart was removed and placed in a silver-gilt locket to be presented to the convent at Chaillot. His brain was placed in a bronze-gilt urn on a monument at the Scots College, a college of the university in Paris. The Scots College was a centre for exiled Scottish Catholics and later a rallying point for sup-porters of James's grandson Bonnie Prince Charlie before he came back to claim the throne in the Jacobite uprising of 1745. Sadly, it was destroyed, and the contents scattered during the French Revolution. James's bowels and viscera were placed in two gilt urns and sent to the parish church of Saint-Germain-en-Laye and the English Jesuit college at Saint-Omer. Strangely the skin from his right arm was given to the English Augustinian nuns of Paris.

What was left of his corpse was placed into a triple sarcoph-agus with two wooden coffins and one of lead. They were taken to St Edmund's Chapel in the Church of the English Benedic-tines in the Rue St Jacques in Paris. The coffins were placed in a side chapel and surrounded by candles that were kept burning in the hope that James might one day be returned to England and buried at Westminster Abbey. They burned until the French Revolution when soldiers came looking for lead to melt down into bullets.

Mr Fitzsimmons, an elderly Irish gentleman, gave an account in 1840 of what he witnessed in Paris, where he was a prisoner during the French Revolution. The sans-culottes, the republican revolutionaries, came looking for the lead and opened James's coffins. The body lay exposed, and he described it as beautiful and perfect. Just as if James was alive. Several wax masks that hung in the chapel must have been James's death masks, as they were very like the corpse Mr Fitzsimmons could now see. He could smell vinegar and camphor from the embalming process. He saw hands and nails that were very fine, and could move each of them freely. 'I never saw so fine a set of teeth in my life'. He tried to extract a tooth, but could not get one out. The sans-culottes took the body, saying that they would bury him in the churchyard, but Fitzsimmons did not know what they did with the King's remains. King George III later enquired about the whereabouts of James's body but found no information.

By the time of his death, James had long since been deposed as king in England and Scotland. His daughter Mary had taken his crown and ruled with her husband William III, but not for long.

Mary II

Died 1694

Mary was the eldest daughter of the slightly scandalous marriage between James II and the commoner Anne Hyde. She saw her mother Anne die of likely breast cancer after becoming morbidly obese, and her father James remarried. A younger half-brother, also James, was born, but the boy was shunned by the Protestant nation along with his father. Mary and her husband were invited to England to take the crown by the Immortal Seven, the most influential men in the land.

Mary's husband was her cousin William, Stadtholder of the Netherlands, though the first time she was told that they were to marry she burst into tears and was inconsolable. She did not want to marry the short ugly Dutchman with an asthma problem and chronic cough. He was twelve years her senior. Eventually she began to feel at home in the Netherlands, she overlooked her husband's infidelities, and they grew fond of each other. Queen Mary came back to England to rule the nation but insisted on having her husband by her side. William had his own distant claim to the throne as well, being a nephew of James II. The solution was a joint monarchy of William and Mary. They were crowned together and held a very serious and dull court where few visitors were allowed. Work was the priority. Their court was a far cry from that of her party-loving Uncle Charles. William spent much time away, fighting off the Jacobites, supporters of the deposed King James. Mary got on with the business of ruling the kingdom in his absence but soon it was William who was left to rule alone.

As with Queen Elizabeth the century before, Mary contracted the tiny virus without any feeling or warning, but she soon started to feel tired and fevered. Fearing the worst, Mary got her affairs in order. She always feared the worst, but this time she was right. She destroyed all the papers that she did not want anyone else to see, burning diary pages and letters. At first it was thought she might have measles, but pustules came to tell a different story. Both of William's parents had died from the smallpox and now it was taking his wife. The King was so upset he moved into her room and slept on a cot beside her, crying through the night. Having survived smallpox himself it was understood that he was unlikely to succumb again. Mary's immune system was humbled by the replication of the virus within her cells. She did not feel too much pain but developed a grossly swollen face. Her skin lesions merged into large areas of dusky red patches and bleeding from the mucous membranes, the linings of the mouth and nose, indicated haemorrhagic smallpox. That she spat blood and had blood-streaked urine would point to that diagnosis also. The toxaemia would have led to multi-organ failure, liver, lungs, heart, kidneys all unable to function under the onslaught of the tiny killer. She died in the early hours of the morning on 28 December 1694. It was a horrendous end for Mary and for those who witnessed her suffering. She was thirty-two years old and after suffering two miscarriages, had no children or an heir of her own.

Queen Mary left a note to say that she did not want her body opened post-mortem. She was ignored and they cut her open anyway for embalming. Let us hope that those who ignored the Queen's request did not get too close to the virus that killed their monarch. She was laid to rest at Westminster Abbey and William wore a lock of her hair close to his heart for the rest of his life.

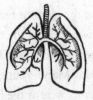

William III

Died 1702

'*Cheers to the little gentleman in the black velvet waistcoat.*'
Popular Jacobean toast

King Billy came from the Netherlands to rule England not just as a nephew of James II, but also as his son-in-law, but he faced mixed reviews.

James II had been facing mounting opposition in England, and he did not help matters by promoting his friends, Catholics, to positions above Anglicans. He alienated everyone around him with his vanity and his increasingly strange policies. He seems to have forgotten his father was beheaded not all that long ago. Syphilis can do strange things to the mind. For many, but not all, it was probably a good thing that he did not put up any sort of resistance when William arrived with his army, ready for a fight.

William had been invited to come and be king with his wife Mary as queen. James got wind of it and decided it was best to slip out the back door, for now, and so the glorious revolution was a success for William and Mary, who were offered the throne jointly. He would have been happy with a regency, but here they were, crowned king and queen of England, with Mary's younger sister Anne named as successor for now. Protestants were at the helm again.

James, once his nosebleed cleared up, did not just disappear completely. He came back to challenge William, first in Ireland. James's challenge was put down by the new king, who was to spend most of his time putting down Catholic and Jacobite revolts. Despite the wins, William was not hugely popular. He was rather dull and his court was dreary and unwelcoming. His spoken English was not exceptional, and he relied heavily on those around him to get work done.

In 1694 Mary felt those tell-tale first signs of the viral illness of smallpox. She was not as lucky as some and succumbed to the awful disease. William even considered abdicating because he was so upset and his health started to get worse. He was always very serious, but now he was just plain miserable without Mary. King Billy was to rule alone for eight years.

William suffered with swollen legs, and haemorrhoids caused him the most terrible pain. Haemorrhoids are painful swellings of the blood vessels at the anus that can cause bleeding. William was thin and small and did a lot of coughing. For years he had suffered from lung problems. He had asthma, a disease where the airways constrict and restrict the movement of air in and out of the lungs. An asthma attack can be terrifying and debilitating, and even fatal. It came as no surprise when William died in 1702 from pneumonia brought on by a traumatic accident.

*   *   *

William III was riding one day, supposedly on a horse that had been stolen from Jacobite enemies. The horse tripped, stumbling on a tiny molehill. William was thrown off and landed on his outstretched arm, a classic mechanism for injury to the clavicle. Upon hitting the ground, the energy shot up his arm. At the top, his collarbone took the full force and snapped in two. The bone was slow to heal, probably not helped by doctors taking blood from their already sickly patient. So, there he was, lying in bed, not moving, feeling very sorry for himself, undergoing the latest in medicinal phlebotomy, when he developed a chest infection and died. Pneumonia, the old man's friend, had come early for William of Orange, who died in the arms of his Dutch physician Govard Bidloo, when he was only fifty-two years old.

The Jacobites, beaten down by the Protestant king in England, Scotland and over the water in Ireland, celebrated when King Billy died and they had a wee mole to thank for it. They celebrated the mole by raising their glasses to the little gentleman in the black velvet waistcoat.

Over the dead body of William III, his two medical men, Bidloo and William Cowper, came to blows. There had been an argument simmering between the two over an accusation of plagiarism. Bidloo had published an anatomy book, *Anatomia Humani Corporis*, in Amsterdam in 1685, but it had not sold well. The publishers sold the plates and Cowper added new text to them, complete with criticisms, which did not go down well. Bidloo called Cowper a highwayman and demanded that The Royal Society kick him out. Now the pair faced each other over the King's frothy pleuritic lung tissue. Sadly, not much was written of it, but the autopsy results were recorded. The fractured collarbone had indeed been setting. The lungs were filled with frothy sputum and the lung tissue was attached to the pleura. They commented on the King's obviously emaciated state and made it clear that William was gravely ill before his fall from the horse.

There was not a huge ceremony at William's funeral, he was buried in haste and not mourned greatly. Big funerals were not really a Stewart thing to do, although he did push the boat out for his wife Mary when she died a few years before. The squabbles amongst his medics continued, mostly over who was responsible for the King's treatment in the months before his death. Over in The Hague whilst inspecting the Dutch armies, the King was seen by eyewitnesses who said he looked 'like a dead man'. He clearly was not well before his horse stumbled on the molehill. The medical men were trying to shift the blame onto each other.

The story goes that William had tied on his left arm a ribbon which held a ring containing some hair belonging to his late wife Mary. Historians had a bit of a spat about it in the mid twentieth century, saying it was all made up. Funny, isn't it, the hills people are prepared to die on.

William and Mary died without having a child of their own as heir. Though it was the primary job of monarchs to provide an heir, neither the Tudors nor the Stewarts were terribly good at it. Instead, as was agreed when the pair came to the throne, despite typical sisterly disputes, it was Mary's younger sister Anne who next took the crown.

Anne

Died 1714

> *'Sleep was never more welcome to a weary traveller than death was to her.'*
>
> Attributed to Dr John Arbuthnot,
> Royal physician, satirist and polymath

Queen Anne is often forgotten. Though her reign was a time for gathering at coffee shops, being seen at the opera and joyful concerts, her personal story is a rather sad one and all because of a mystery underlying medical condition. Queen Anne had seventeen pregnancies and yet when she died, she, as many monarchs before her, died without an heir to pass the crown on to.

Born the second daughter of James II, it was unlikely that Anne would be queen. How many times have we made that claim so far? As a child she was self-doubting, eager to please and had a well-known stubborn streak (a phrase that seems only ever to be used when talking about women). She was incredibly near-sighted and suffered from 'defluxion' of the eyes. The constant watering required medical attention before she was even five years old. She was constantly blushing and often used make-up to cover her blotchy skin.

Anne and her older sister Mary, heir presumptive, were pushed down the pecking order when James II remarried and had a son, James. Rumours, fuelled by Anne, claimed an infant had been brought in to pretend to be the new heir, fitting anti-Catholic rhetoric. She didn't like her half-brother James much.

James and his son were deposed in favour of Mary, with Anne designated her heir, should Mary not have children. Anne expected her services would not be required, but became queen when William died in 1702. Anne was married to Prince George of Denmark, who by all accounts was even more dull than her brother-in-law William. He also suffered with a sickly chest and his heavy breathing was sometimes the only sign he was even alive. Together they could have produced the next monarch, but Anne had medical complications that struck again and again. Of her seventeen pregnancies, many were miscarried and only three children survived beyond a few days. Two girls succumbed to smallpox and her son William, Duke of Gloucester, died when only eleven years old.

William suffered from fits, though they were not well described, and he had a strange swelling at the back of his head. Doctors aspirated fluid from the swelling, likely cerebro-spinal fluid, that would have escaped from a defect within the skull. Draining off the CSF was dangerous. Sticking needles into the tissues would have risked infection of the linings of the brain. The day after the boy turned eleven, he complained of a sore throat with nausea, fever and diarrhoea. He had short, broken sleep and became delirious. He also developed a rash which at first was thought might be another case of smallpox. Famed physician John Radcliffe was sent for. Although he had been credited with saving young William's life when he was three years old, he had fallen out of favour with the Queen on account of his liking a drink. Now they needed all the help they could get but it was futile. The famous doctor could not help and the boy died a few days later. An autopsy described his swollen neck and inflamed structures within. There was no mention of smallpox or measles or scarlet fever: all diseases that his physicians would have been familiar with. Instead, his death was described as being due to 'malignant fever'. There was much dispute over the death of William, with far-reaching consequences for succession plans and the future of the nation. Anne was understandably heartbroken. Her inability to produce an heir was not for want of trying.

Anne's reign is chiefly remembered for the Act of the Union between England and Scotland in 1707, for the victory over the French at Blenheim in 1704, and because Anne was the last of the Stewart monarchs. Much is also made of her relationship with Sarah Churchill, who was hugely influential given her closeness to the Queen. They may have been lovers and their letters to each other give away rather a lot. They had pet names for each other: Anne was Mrs Morley and Sarah, Mrs Freeman.

As for her illness, Queen Anne may well have had lupus erythematosus – an autoimmune condition during which something unknown triggers the immune system to create antibodies against parts of itself. Antibodies grab hold of unrecognised entities and act as flags for the immune system to identify and attack. Lupus has an array of common symptoms and Anne suffered from many of them.

She suffered what was described as gout, a condition commonly blamed on wine and rich foods. Anne did indeed like too much strong wine but gout is rare in young, pre-menopausal women and tended to affect only one joint. The Queen had pain and swelling in more than one of her joints and so it sounds more like Anne suffered a polyarthritis. The flare-ups coincided with the rashes on her face, another symptom that also points towards lupus. Autoantibodies could be the cause of the miscarriages, along with the symptoms of skin-blotching polyarthritis, kidney damage and oedema.

Through it all Anne kept comfort-eating and drinking. One could hardly blame her for that with so many pregnancies ending in tragedy and two daughters dying from smallpox. Dissenters and Jacobites nicknamed her Brandy Nan on account of her fondness for drink. Her health deteriorated. She put on more weight and suffered terribly with the consequences. Anne even needed to be carried on a chair to her own coronation, unable to walk, suffering an attack of arthritis, often referred to as gout.

In 1714 Anne had a series of strokes. As she lay on her deathbed her skin was intentionally blistered using hot irons, the blister fluid was then drained in a bid to balance the humours. Emetics were given, inducing vomiting for the same purpose. Her head was shaved and garlic pressed against her feet. Blood was removed and prayers were said. She died on the first day of August in

1714. She was forty-nine years old. John Arbuthnot, one of the physicians who signed the post-mortem report, wrote in a letter to Jonathan Swift, 'I believe sleep was never more welcome to a weary traveller than death was to her.'

Dr Thomas Lawrence performed a post-mortem of sorts in the act of embalming the body. He noted a small umbilical hernia without any excoriation, and a large omentum (the fat and connective tissue that covers the abdominal organs). They found the stomach wall to be thin with an inward lining much smoother than it should be. They described an ulcer on her leg. There are other thoughts, of course, congenital syphilis being one (her father James likely died of the disease), but lupus remains top of the differential diagnosis considering Anne's systemic symptoms and her obstetric tragedies. Despite her attempts, there were no Stewarts left to keep the dynasty alive.

The last of the Stewarts lay in state at Kensington Palace for three weeks. Her body was then placed in a coffin draped in purple, and she was interred in the Stewart vault at Westminster Abbey Lady Chapel. She lies there with her husband, her sister Mary and Mary's husband William III, as well as their uncle Charles II and some of her infant children who died shortly after birth. Distant cousin Georg Ludwig of Hanover was invited to come over to England and claim his crown.

George I

Died 1727

Queen Anne's death had the potential to leave a big Protestant-sized hole behind. Under the Act of Settlement of 1701 and after the death of her only surviving son, there would be no Protestant heir to the throne ahead of at least fifty Catholic claimants. This was problematic. The next Protestant in line, from miles away in Germany, was Sophia, Electress of Hanover. She died only two months before Queen Anne, leaving her son, His Highness Duke Georg Ludwig of Brunswick-Lunenberg as heir. He, for some reason, had a little difficulty in speaking English. Nevertheless he was not a Catholic, and that was what mattered to the English. George was informed of the death of Anne and he caught the next boat to his new kingdom.

James Stewart, son of James II and nicknamed the Old Pretender by the Whigs, was not going to sit back and see his throne taken by some far-flung Protestant Hanoverian. He sent requests to Anne to be considered as her heir but they were ignored. He landed in Scotland and raised supporters amongst the clans of the north. In 1715 at Braemar, Jacobite supporter the Earl of Mar raised the standard of King James VIII of Scotland and James III of England. The uprising and Mar's men were put down. George faced much Jacobite opposition during his reign, sponsored by the many enemies of Hanover and by Catholics at home and abroad. This was not the end of the rebellion (or you might call it an uprising, depending on which side you were on).

George I's twelve-year reign had it all. Tension, intrigue, family feuding, political corruption and bribery. George was not popular, nobody knew who he was and he spent most of his time elsewhere whilst Walpole and the politicians ran the country. He had a huge falling-out with his son and threw him out of court. With his own wife imprisoned for alleged adultery, George brought two mistresses with him to England. Neither were considered to be attractive and were made fun of in society, nicknamed The Maypole and The Elephant. The Hanoverians brought corruption and bribery over in barge loads. Controlling the newspapers and using them for the considered management of public opinion is not a new idea by any means. Even the prime minister Robert Walpole at first bribed and later bought the *London Journal* to put an end to criticisms of his government.

In 1723, when he was sixty-three years old, George suffered a stroke that left him senseless for an hour. He recovered fully but it was a sign of things to come. He continued to travel back and forth from Britain to the Continent. In 1727 he embarked on yet another of many trips to Hanover, but this was to be his last. The crossing and the first part of his journey were uneventful

246

but soon the jolting of the carriage, a large meal of fruit and a frustrating letter from his imprisoned wife unsettled the King. He complained of an upset stomach and stopped the carriage to attend a call of nature. On his return, it was noticed that the King's face had become strangely distorted and that he was struggling to use his right hand. A surgeon was called, and he quickly diagnosed a stroke.

They moved George to lie on some grass and bled him immediately. Some smelling salts brought him back to consciousness and they drove on, but his symptoms worsened. Another stop and this time, the doctors applied plasters to his hands, they gave him strong spirits and they bled him some more. Inside the King's skull, in the vulnerable soft tissue of the brain, cells were dying as they were starved of oxygen by a clot or a bleed. Cell necrosis is followed by a leak of their contents, causing damage to surrounding neurons. In the King's brain there would be an immune response to the injury, causing inflammation, failure of the energy systems, acidosis, and impairment of the blood–brain barrier. To block the blood through cerebral blood vessels is dangerous.

As they drove on in the carriage to Osnabrück, the King slept a quite 'unnatural sleep with deep snoring'. He was carried up a secret staircase to avoid publicity and put to bed. 'I'm done,' he said and took his last breath. He was sixty-seven years old.

Though the signs and symptoms of stroke were obvious to his physicians, there was no way to determine if the King's death had been due to a clot causing ischaemia or a haemorrhage on his brain, without directly examining his brain tissue after a dissection. He ordered that his body was not to be cut open nor embalmed, and unlike with Queen Mary II's very same request, this one was not ignored.

He was not brought back to England but buried at Osnabrück. During the Second World War George I's tomb was damaged and his sarcophagus and that of his mother were moved to a later-built mausoleum in Herrenhausen Gardens in Hanover where it remains today. His son George was next to wear the crown in a reign that strangely mirrored his father's.

George II

Died 1760

The new king, George, was the second of the four successive Georges. Each one became slightly more English and less Hanoverian than the last, but like his father, this George spoke mostly German and spent more time worrying about Hanover than England, Scotland and Ireland.

Walpole, keen to keep on the right side of the monarchy, and keep his job, scrambled to be first to tell the King that his father had died suddenly during his continental travels. George had fought so much with his father that he imagined it was some sort of trick. Not quite believing that he had actually died, he thought it all a ruse to incite him into treason from his place beyond the court.

George II came to the throne in 1727. It was a time of giant wigs and flamboyantly tightly covered calf muscles topped with garters. It was also a time of exceptionally grumpy Hanoverians. Portraits of George II might leave you concerned about his thyroid function in light of his exophthalmos eyes, even though they have been pushed in by painters, eager not to upset the bulgy-eyed king.

Some contemporary accounts described George II as a feeble fool. He was critical of everybody and everything around him. He was judgemental and aggressive. Unsurprisingly, nobody liked him much. The King did not like the English, to him they were regicides who had it in for their monarchs. His hatred was not solely for England, he also hated his eldest son, Prince Frederick. He was not manly enough, and was far too fond of music. 'Kids today,' George II would say with enormous bulging eye-rolls. George himself had no interest in the arts or the sciences. He felt his own son was weak for loving the arts and playing the cello.

Frederick courted the popularity that his father did not have. He overtly drank gin in public bars when the Gin Act of 1736 tried to put a stop to it. The prince failed to inform his parents when his wife was due to give birth and the news was hidden from them. Going against protocol, he upset them greatly. This resulted in George thowing his son out and banishing him from court, despite the birth of a new heir, young Prince George.

It was all a rerun of George I, with George II's bickering with his son and heir, although this time, the son died before he could become king. After being struck in the chest by a cricket ball or maybe a real tennis ball, Frederick died at only forty-four years old.

George II's popularity did increase somewhat when he went to the Continent and excitedly took command of allied armies at Dettingen during the War of the Austrian Succession. He was the last British monarch to do so; though others since have been involved in war efforts, they were not on their horse at the front, wielding their swords and excitedly rallying the troops.

The Jacobites rose up in the north again, in favour of the Catholic Stewarts' claim to the throne. George's other son, the Duke of Cumberland, was sent to Scotland where he finally defeated the Jacobites at the Battle of Culloden, near Inverness in 1746. There was no need for George to risk his life again by fighting on the windswept northern moor.

In November 1737 Queen Caroline, George II's wife, died of a strangulated umbilical hernia. Her naval became weakened during her last pregnancy and later a loop of bowel pushed itself out through the weakness in the wall. It became cut off from its blood supply from within the abdomen. Necrosis followed, with peritonitis and obstruction. She kept quiet about the hernia, telling nobody. George was grumpy and became irritated by her vomiting. Eventually the surgeons got a look and after much discussion they decided that they must operate. They did not free the strangulated bowel but merely stuck a knife into the protrusion and allowed the foul contents to drain. Unsurprisingly, gangrene set in and Caroline died. As she lay dying she told her husband that he should find another wife. No, he said, but I will take mistresses if that's OK. In his seventies, hard of hearing and blind in one eye, the King's libido remained as enormous as his wigs, and at his funeral his many mistresses were inconsolable.

George awoke on 25 October 1760 and in keeping with his military precision he had his usual hot chocolate (how very continental) and took himself off to his bathroom for his morning ablutions. The valet recalled that he heard a noise that was 'louder than the Royal wind' coming from the bathroom. Hats off to the man whose job it was to distinguish between the sound of the royal wind, and other suspicious noises. The valet found the King slumped on the bathroom floor, breeches round his ankles. He was still alive but gravely unwell. They dragged him back to his bed, but he did not recover. Before the Princess Emelia could arrive at his bedside, the King was dead. George II died in 1760, struck down whilst on the throne, whilst on the throne. He was seventy-six years old.

His post-mortem revealed a thoracic aortic dissection, which had spontaneously burst under the pressure of his toilet trip. It is not unusual for someone to die suddenly whilst on the toilet. It is, after all, a highly pressurised environment.

Dr Frank Nicholls was the King's physician who was directed to open and embalm the body. He meticulously described what he found. The organs of the abdomen were normal, as were the brain and the lungs. Nearly a pint of coagulated blood was found within the distended pericardium. The blood that had got inside this sac that surrounds the heart had constricted the organ. The ventricles, squeezed so hard, had all the blood squeezed out of them. A large transverse (sideways) fissure on the trunk of the aorta measured about an inch and a half long, through which the blood had passed, causing an 'elevated ecchymosis'. So the aorta, the large vessel that carries the newly oxygenated blood under pressure away from the heart, had a tear in it; the blood poured through the gash and gathered around the heart, causing a tamponade. It squeezed his heart to death.

George II

This is thought to be the first description of an aortic dissection and it is so thorough. Nicholls wrote it all in a letter to the Royal Society with an in-depth description of the anatomy and the events. The man who first classified the disease of aortic aneurysms was a cardiovascular surgeon called Dr Michael DeBakey. For DeBakey, who suffered an aortic dissection himself in 2005, his work saved his own life. His team performed on their teacher the very surgery he had pioneered, and he lived to two months shy of his one-hundredth birthday. DeBakey developed the surgical procedure that could have saved George II's life, unfortunately 300 years too late.

George II was buried at Westminster Abbey, the last of the English monarchs to be interred there. His coffin was placed with his wife Queen Caroline who had died two decades before. George had asked that the sides of Caroline's coffin be removed so that their remains may be able to mingle. His heir Frederick had already died, but not before having a son of his own to carry on the direct line. The Hanoverians were better at ensuring succession. A young George took up the crown as George III.

George III

Died 1820

Courtiers looked on in horror in 1788 as their king conversed with a tree. He even shook its hand, believing the tree to be the king of Prussia. He was foaming at the mouth, talking until hoarse and acting incredibly inappropriately and obscenely towards women in court. This was just one frightening episode in which King George III lost his mind. When the King could not deliver his speech at the opening of Parliament that year, prime minister William Pitt and opposing senior Whig Charles James Fox debated a regency. Even the very existence of monarchy itself was once again up for debate. George III had been on the throne for fifty-nine years, during a time of considerable change and upheaval for the country, but his reign is chiefly remembered for the mental state of the king who went mad and ended his days shut away from the world, blind, deaf and slowly dying of dementia.

George III's father Frederick had died in 1751, and so George inherited from his grandfather George II. He not only inherited the throne, of course, but also his bulging blue eyes and a vigorous need to be judgemental of everyone. The love of arts and music though, he got from his father Frederick. George would much rather have run far away from his position as king, yet he became the longest-reigning monarch England and Scotland had seen.

George III made a promising start. He was a conscientious, able and dedicated king. He was also slightly unusual for the Hanoverians, in that he was faithful to his wife. His family's antics were a completely different story. He had a brother Edward who died of syphilis at only twenty-eight years old. His brother Henry was disgraced by his sexual misadventures. His sister Caroline was imprisoned for adultery in Denmark. It was George who steadied the ship, dutifully marrying Charlotte of Mecklenburg-Strelitz and together they had thirteen children. As a young man George III was described as vain and obstinate, prone to sulkiness and behaving like a child. Though less likely to rock the boat like his siblings, there's no doubt that he had Hanoverian genes. His predecessors were a cantankerous bunch and he carried on with the family trait.

There was so much about George's long reign that could have challenged his health. The not-so-small matter of losing the American colonies for a start. The British taxed them too much, particularly on the essentials of paper and tea, and yet the colonies had no say in Parliament in Britain. During the Boston Tea Party enough tea was thrown into the harbour to send anyone British over the edge. The response from Britain was not to start talking over a table set for two, but rather further clamping down. The colonists were not going to be given any autonomy and were now in open defiance. Losing the American colonies was such a blow. George III actually wrote his letter of abdication but thought twice before pressing send. We've all been there, George.

Some say that it was George's fits of insanity that brought about the loss. Others say that the loss brought on his madness. There was a short attack of his illness in 1765 but it was kept quiet, and he recovered quickly. In 1788 George had his first alarming physical attack. Certainly, it was more physical in nature than psychiatric, characterised by debilitating pains in his abdomen and uncontrollable diarrhoea. His pains were described as 'biliary' by his physician. Biliary refers to the gallbladder and the pains one might get with an acute cholecystitis or cholangitis (inflammation of the gallbladder or the bile ducts), but the other symptoms of limb weakness and emotional agitation baffled those around him. The episode was bad enough to be given a name of its own: 'The Cheltenham attack'. George had been sent to Cheltenham to take the waters and recover, but a few months after returning he felt his heart racing once again. When the Prince of Wales visited his ill father, the sight made him burst into tears, enticing the King to attack his son, throwing him against a wall. 'I am not ill,' he said, 'but I am nervous.' He went on to hold imaginary parades and talk to long-dead old friends.

During the next attack George suffered constipation, darkening of the urine (an important observation in the future posthumous diagnoses of the King's madness), limb weakness, hoarseness and a fast pulse. He became increasingly restless with headaches and visual disturbances. He became delirious and he started having convulsions. On one occasion he fell into a pro-longed stupor. Lucid restful moments were sandwiched between crazed excitability. His physicians' remedies were having no effect. They placed leeches on his body. With three jaws and one hundred teeth, leeches bite through the layers of skin. Their saliva then baths the site in an anticoagulant that allows the blood to flow freely. They suck out the blood to feed themselves and in the process were thought to bring balance. The doctors tried cupping, scolding, feet plasters, bleeding and emetics, all designed to draw out fluids and thus rebalance the humours.

When it was accepted that the remedies were having no effect, the famous Dr Francis Willis, specialist in treating mental disorders, was called for. He had a very different view of matters. The King was given both castor oil and laudanum, no doubt leaving the poor man's bowels completely baffled over what course to take. He was restrained with ropes and a straitjacket, the idea being that inflicting such suffering would most certainly lead to a change in behaviour. If his patients did not do as Willis instructed, they were met with sanctions the brutality of which we find hard to swallow today.

In 1789, as the streets of Paris were rocked by revolution, Britain's King George recovered from his illness. A few years later the French king Louis XVI lost his head to the guillotine, but George's remained attached, and functioning, for now. In 1800 George faced a would-be assassin who shot at him at close range but missed. The King's composure under fire did a lot of good for his popularity.

Though his grandfather George II is remembered as being

258

the last of the monarchs to lead troops in battle, George III was well prepared to do so. If Napoleon decided to cross the Channel and invade England, the King was ready to meet his advances. His popularity improved even more, on the eastern side of the Atlantic at least.

Sadly, delirious attacks returned in 1804. There was a recovery, but another attack came in 1810 after the death of his daughter Amelia. In early 1811 it was necessary for Parliament to pass a regency bill so that the Prince of Wales became Prince Regent. This time there was no recovery. The onset of dementia meant that the King was kept out of sight at Windsor; he would not play a part in British life again.

In 1969 a theory was published by mother-and-son team Macalpine and Hunter that has captured the collective imagination. The rare genetic metabolic disorder porphyria could provide an explanation for George's condition. Porphyria is a group of diseases that interrupt the production of heam. Heam makes the haemoglobin within the red blood cells. Porphyrins, which are normally used in the process, instead build up causing an array of symptoms. These can include muscle soreness, abdominal pains and numbness as well as mania, depression and hallucinations. Porphyria derives from the Greek for purple, a description of the alarming blue-purple urine produced by sufferers of the disease as the colourful porphyrins find their way out.

Medical conditions of relatives may also have suggested that the family were passing on this rare disorder. Queen Caroline Matilda of Norway and Denmark, Prince Frederick's daughter, died in 1775 of a mystery illness. She was only twenty-three years old. Her illness featured a rapidly progressive paralysis. When such a thing happens the spreading paralysis will eventually reach the muscles of the chest wall and breathing will become impossible. Death will very quickly follow. Other records claim she died of scarlet fever and was lucid enough on her deathbed to write to her brother claiming her innocence over accusations of a scandalous affair. There is not an obvious connection to make between her death and the disease porphyria though.

The claim made that George IV's gout and Princess Charlotte's death in childbirth were also due to porphyria are a bit far-fetched. These can be explained by far more common pathological processes. It is strange though, that none of the twentieth or twenty-first-century royals have suffered from the disease. It is not as if the royal genetics have been kept from the prying eyes of the public for the last two hundred years. Queen Victoria's familial haemophilia was well documented.

Macalpine and Hunter made a strong argument for porphyria but evidence of other royals and illegitimates suffering from the disease was just not there. Citing that Mary, Queen of Scots and James VI/I were prone to colic is not strong enough. Opponents of the porphyria theory have demonstrated that some of the medications given to the King are well known to turn the urine blue. Another piece to the puzzle was that a lock of the King's hair was later tested and found to contain high levels of the poison arsenic. Yes, the porphyria theorists will say, arsenic can trigger acute porphyria attacks. No, the opponents will reply, arsenic can make anyone sick regardless of porphyria.

An alternative argument won out for a while, that losing the

American colonies caused the King's ill health. There were also prominent historians in the 1960s who suggested that George had simply gone mad because he could find no relief in tensions brought about by being married to an ugly wife. This says far more about the historians than George's health.

Poring over George's letters, recent researchers have revealed fascinating correlations. During his so-called mad periods, his colourful language and the structure of his never-ending sentences reveal a patient in the manic phase of a bipolar disorder. This is not due to the rare genetic disorder of porphyria, they say, but simply bipolar disorder (not that it is ever that simple). Bipolar disorder is not simply a relapsing psychological disorder, there can also be physical manifestations of abdominal symptoms, muscular pains and weakness. Whilst the relationship between bipolar disorder and frontotemporal dementia is not known exactly, a link is recognised, and the progression is being researched. There appear to be shared molecular mechanisms and it could be that George's bipolar disorder did not kill him directly, but it progressed to a dementia that slowly took his life.

As ever, retrospective diagnosis, whilst fun, is not exact and we are left with different possibilities. For George there were no answers and his intermittent attacks evolved into dementia. He was unaware when a coalition army at Waterloo defeated the threat of Napoleon once and for all in June of 1815. He was not lucid enough to be involved and the bumbling Prince Regent took the credit. The King was not aware when his wife Charlotte died in 1818.

On the evening of 29 January 1820, the King's suffering ended.

He died at eighty-one, the longest reigning of the monarchs to that date. After a considerable wait, the Prince Regent became King George IV. He took vanity to a whole new level, rebelling against his father's dull morality.

George IV

Died 1830

After ten years as Prince Regent while his father slowly died of dementia, George's own reign lasted only another ten years. In that time he suffered all manner of illnesses, a long list of mostly non-communicable conditions that were the result of his lavish, over-the-top kind of life. George was caricatured in the press as a large, morally devoid prince of excess. Distilling his final diagnosis down into a simple conclusion is not possible. Gambling, drinking and debauchery helped George IV to compete for the title of worst of all the monarchs.

George, eldest son of George III, was nothing like his rather plain father. Instead he was flamboyant and vain. He covered himself in fashionable finery and delighted in the arts. He liked a drink, and he liked the girls just as much. Scandal and gossip followed Prince George everywhere and cost his father dearly in his purse and in stress.

In 1785 George secretly married his love of the moment, a

Catholic widow called Maria Fitzherbert. His father, who would never have given permission for such a marriage, persuaded the prince, again by opening his purse, to marry a more suitable candidate and his marriage to Maria Fitzherbert was deemed illegal and invalid. George, who relented once his eye-wateringly large debts were paid off, married Caroline of Brunswick. George and Caroline had one legitimate child, Princess Charlotte. George detested his wife. She died three weeks after his coronation, but he was not the least bit upset.

The year 1810 was a difficult time. The King had lost his mind, Napoleon was rampaging through Europe and there was the whiff of republicanism in the air. The disliked Prince George was named Regent. When he finally donned the crown in 1820, George IV set off to visit those parts of the kingdom that had been long ignored by his father. He was the first monarch to visit Ireland since 1690. In Scotland his waistline needed a considerable length of fabric to wear the tartan that had been banned by his great-grandfather and he enjoyed a glass or two of the best of the whiskies from Glenlivet.

At the end of his life, George IV had quite a few medical troubles, or a 'mixed pathology' as one might say at a medical conference. The famed surgeon Sir Astley Cooper carried out a post-mortem on the lifeless large body of the King. It would have been a long day at the office for the doctor.

Cooper's findings demonstrated the lifetime of lavish excess that King George IV enjoyed. Chronic, lifestyle-related conditions are the primary killers of Queen Elizabeth II's subjects today and many of us are undergoing modern treatments for the ailments that affected George IV. Obesity, myocardial and valvular heart disease, fatty liver, portal hypertension, a gastric diverticulum, and stones in his bladder all affected the King's health. These are the results of what George consumed throughout his life and together they brought about his end. No dagger in an orifice, or poleaxe through the head. The monarchs were no longer risking their lives leading charging troops in battle or concerning themselves with the threat of poison. George was lucky enough to avoid the extreme mental ill-health that took his father. He avoided so many of the lethal infectious diseases that took his predecessors too. George even managed to escape losing his head despite the waves of republicanism across the Channel. With George, we've entered the modern period of chronic lifestyle-related ill health. For the monarchs to come there was going to be less of a threat from infection and more the threat of lifestyle and excess. In this way, the manner of their deaths reflected the future health of the nation. Beyond famine and war, the monarchs' deaths were a sign of things to come for everyone.

George IV was keen on attending the opening of the tombs of his ancestors and inspecting their remains, but his own body lies so far undisturbed. He is buried in St George's Chapel vault at Windsor. At his funeral his successor and brother William was so excited about becoming king that he behaved in a most undignified manner, giggling and making comments like a child even though he was sixty-five years old.

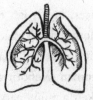

Princess Charlotte

Died 1817

Princess Charlotte was the only legitimate child of George IV and Caroline of Brunswick and as such, was his heir. In November 1817 she was twenty years old and quite well. She took her first pregnancy to term and had a baby boy, but within five hours, the princess was dead. The baby did not survive either. The obstetrician, Sir Richard Croft, faced such a backlash that he took his own life.

Speculation and posthumous diagnosis were that Princess Charlotte died of a postpartum haemorrhage, but more recent analysis of the accounts has drawn different conclusions. In 1988 Andrew Friedman et al. at Yale Obstetrics Department noted there were no contemporary accounts of excessive external bleeding, which does not match the diagnosis. An autopsy report declared that there was a blood clot in her uterus, but it was not big enough to have caused death by internal blood loss. So, why a diagnosis of haemorrhage? It must have been based on observations of the princess in her last moments, but there are other clues about Charlotte's death that we can interpret with a modern lens. Accounts suggested that Charlotte had acute respiratory distress. Friedman, Kohorn and Nuland concluded that this was far more likely a pulmonary embolism. Pulmonary embolism was a condition not described before 1846 and so the doctor Richard Croft would not have known of the danger.

Charlotte's pulmonary embolism was a clot that had developed within distant blood vessels and made its way through the vasculature to her lungs. There it clogged the pulmonary vessels and prevented blood from getting through for oxygenation at the lung interface. Within moments of giving birth, Charlotte was gasping for air. She gulped, trying to pull more air into the lungs to give her tissues the oxygen they needed, but it was no good. The oxygen could not get through, the blood was being stopped by the clot.

Even today, diagnosing pulmonary embolism is a tricky business. A deep vein thrombosis develops in some distal blood vessel, detaches, embolises and is dragged off with the flow of blood towards the pulmonary circulation. Sometimes evidence of the deep vein thrombosis can be seen in the lower legs with swelling, redness, heat, and pain of the calf – the four classic signs of inflammation.

Large emboli become wedged in the main pulmonary artery and smaller emboli sneak through to become lodged in smaller peripheral lung arteries. Big clots obstructing the pulmonary arteries create dead space ventilation where alveolar ventilation exceeds pulmonary blood flow. The oxygen is getting into the lungs from the outside but there is no blood there to pick it up. Similarly there is no chance of any carbon dioxide being carried by the blood to get through and escape to the outside.

The pressure in the pulmonary artery starts to rise and the backlog puts pressure on the heart's right ventricle. Right ventricular failure can follow. The problem can progress to myocardial ischaemia (lack of oxygen delivery to the muscle of the heart). If the heart cannot do its job and pump blood it will sink into electromechanical dissociation and sudden death. Though that description does not sound sudden, to an onlooker Princess Charlotte's death was immediate. They would have seen her gasping for air, attempting twenty, thirty, or even more breaths per minute to try to provide more oxygen. The heart rate races to try to provide more oxygenated blood to the tissues, even though no new oxygen is getting through. The production of lactic acid is increased. Charlotte may have felt agonising chest pain. She would have turned blue, especially around her mouth. Her hands would turn the tell-tale dusky purple as she passed away.

Of course, these symptoms are not unique to a pulmonary embolism and the critically ill princess could easily have been diagnosed with bleeding internally. A pulmonary embolism does not explain the death of her baby son either. That remains a mystery.

William IV

Died 1837

You could be forgiven for forgetting about William IV, the Sailor King. He was not the most memorable of monarchs, following on from the four Georges with all their family drama. From the start William was not a likely candidate for the throne. Born the third son of George III and Queen Charlotte in 1765, he was not even Duke of York, but the Duke of Clarence. He kept the throne warm for seven years though, before it was Queen Victoria's turn.

William did not become king until he was sixty-five years old and for most of his life he was not preparing for the moment. His chances of ever being king were diminished further when his big brother George had a daughter, Charlotte. Sadly Charlotte died in childbirth, along with her son. There were no other children and so George's heir became his brother Edward, the Duke of York. But Edward died whilst George was king and so William, Duke of Clarence became heir to the throne.

As a boy, William much admired his wayward older brother George and it looked like he might develop George's attitude to life. He was sent away to sea, for his own good. At the age of fourteen he was enrolled as a midshipman on the ship *The Prince George* and sailed off into the sunset towards a life of Navy discipline. The late eighteenth century allowed for William to see combat at sea, and he became a respected officer. Despite the discipline, William enjoyed the life of a sailor with all that involved. Many complained about the rough, swearing, gambling Prince William. After wrecking a brothel in Barbados his father was sent a hefty bill for the damage. His time at sea had not had quite the effect his father intended.

Whenever William returned to England he fell madly in love with someone deemed not worthy by his father and he was sent back to sea. Eventually he settled with an actress called Dorothea Bland and together they had ten illegitimate children. He had to give them up though and make a match deemed more appropriate. He married Princess Adelaide of Saxe-Meiningen and life became rather less fun. The young, loud, brash midshipman became a much gentler, thoughtful, middle-aged heir to the throne. He became king when he was sixty-five and reigned for only seven years. Not that he didn't have his moments. He was known for walking into a bar and ordering champagne all round, insisting that everyone raise their glasses to all manner of toasts. He could be a bit of a bore and it was noted the prince 'exhibited oddities'. Whether that was caused by a genetic propensity for George III's madness via bipolar disorder or by porphyria or syphilis picked up in a brothel, William was noted to have his stranger moments.

There was still no identification of the bacteria that caused the syphilitic destruction of James II and there was, as yet, no antibiotic cure. Instead, those who suffered from the disease had mercury. There is no mention of William having suffered from syphilis but he was well known to have frequented the brothels of the West Indies and the south coast of England as a sailor in his youth. He had a girl in every port, and it is quite possible that he had contracted something that could lead to his difficulties in later life.

In 1837 William's health took a turn for the worse. It became difficult for him to breathe on occasion and he required a wheelchair. He developed heart failure. Before, when it looked like he might become king, he was determined to outlive his brother and he did so. Now he was sick, he became determined to outlive his hated sister-in-law who had control of his young heiress. If he lived long enough, his niece Alexandrina might reach eighteen before he died and would be queen without the interfering regency of her mother. Worse than that was the influence of her mother's private secretary, the controlling John Conroy. Other royals took exception to Conroy's role, calling him 'King John'. William lived long enough to deny them the power of regency, but his lungs had become infected with bacteria that replicated, and the immune cells that tried to gobble them up produced pus that filled his lungs and prevented the movement of gases across his lung cell walls. As tissues start to get sticky and push together, the downward spiral is hard to stop. His physicians surely reacted by bleeding him, removing a portion of much-needed blood. The dying wish of the King was to see another anniversary of the Battle of Waterloo. He made it to the date but was not in good enough health to attend any celebrations. The old man's friend pneumonia carried off another mortal monarch. He died two days later at Windsor Castle on 20 June 1837. He was seventy-one years old.

Some doctors were upset by the news from the King's physicians in the days before his death, which suggests that everything was just fine – until it wasn't. The body was dissected by the famous surgeon of the day, Sir Astley Cooper, who had also dissected the King's brother George. Cooper found a cirrhosis of the enlarged liver and that the King's spleen had grown to twice the size they would have expected. He also found the lung tissue to be filled with mucus, blood and serous fluid. The heart valves were calcified to such an extent that the pathology must have affected function. So, William died of pneumonia on a background of worsening heart and liver failure. No mention was made of any findings in William's brain, which leaves us, as ever, only able to speculate as to his cognitive decline in later years. He had moments where those around him were worried for his mental health but that's not to say that he inherited his father's well-documented mental illness.

Queen Victoria was awoken by news that Lord Conyngham, the Lord Chamberlain, and the Archbishop of Canterbury had arrived, seeking an audience. They brought her the news that her uncle had expired just after 2 a.m. Now, she was the Queen.

Victoria

Died 1901

'I should like to live a little longer as I have a few things to settle.'

Queen Victoria as reported by her
personal physician, Dr James Reid

The enduring image of the icon Queen Elizabeth I is colourful, lavish and bejewelled, but Queen Victoria could not be more different. Mostly remembered in her plain black mourning attire, this queen was iconic for other reasons.

In the late nineteenth century Queen Victoria became Britain's longest-reigning monarch. She first sat on the throne at only eighteen years old and kept the seat warm for even longer than her grandfather George III. It was not looking so good for the Queen into the new century. Victoria was eighty-one years old on Sunday, 3 January 1901, when she made her very last diary entry after sixty-five years of jotting down her daily thoughts. Within the month this grandmother of Europe was dead.

Christmas as ever had been spent at Osborne House on the Isle of Wight. Too bothered with rheumatism to walk, Victoria was confined to a wheelchair. She was weak and also troubled with cataracts. There were no new surgeries or medical discoveries of recent years that could help her now. Throughout her life Queen Victoria had made use of the new ideas coming from surgeons and physicians who were now treating the art of medicine with more scientific endeavour. Early in her life her mother allowed for a young Victoria, or Alexandrina as she was known, to have the smallpox vaccination. Later, she was anaesthetised with chloroform when her last two children were born.

Surgeons understood that suppuration of wounds after a surgical procedure could be a killer and so when Victoria invited surgeon Joseph Lister to her castle at Balmoral in Scotland to deal with a huge abscess in her armpit, he brought his carbolic spray to use on the wound. This new idea came with risks and potential side effects. Luckily for everyone, and especially Lister, the only side effects this time were knighthoods and medals for the physicians and surgeons who successfully treated the Queen.

On 14 December 1861 Prince Albert died, likely of typhoid, though he too had an underlying abdominal disorder that ensured the infection finished him off. Queen Victoria reigned without her husband for forty years until her own death in 1901.

There are different accounts of Victoria's death and none of them overly dramatic. She may have suffered a cerebral haemorrhage after a series of small strokes, but others said that she had cardiac failure, yet another that she simply faded away. Brewer recorded that her death was due to senile decay. Doctors now can still claim Old Age as a cause of death on a death certificate, but there needs to be a thorough examination of the other potential causes of death first. At eighty-one years old, it may well have been any of these conditions that killed the Queen, or more likely a combination, considering that she was in her eighties.

Stroke is the deficit in neurological function that we have seen a number of times now with our mortal monarchs. Any short-lived loss of function is referred to as a transient ischaemic attack. Deficits that last longer than a day are known as cerebrovascular events or stroke. Smaller occlusions can impact on functions like memory, leading to cognitive decline, for instance, but small strokes accumulate. As we saw with Henry III and Edward III, so too with Victoria. William Osler's observation rings true again, that when it comes to this sort of aged decline, 'people take as long to die as they did to grow up.'

It will not come as a surprise to hear that Queen Victoria died of a stroke at the age of eighty-one, or of cardiac failure, which was also suggested. As age increases, so does the propensity for both. Pneumonia too becomes more likely – it had claimed her uncle William IV all those years before. Though Victoria had survived multiple half-hearted attempts on her life, she was not likely to die on the battlefield or from an arrow in the forest whilst out hunting. The greatest threat for her was one few of her predecessors faced: childbirth. Victoria survived childbirth nine times.

There is now an array of treatments for the diseases that

Victoria faced in her ninth decade. We treat pneumonia with a range of antibiotics and even mechanical ventilation. We blow holes in cerebrovascular occlusions with clot-busting drugs. We stent heart vessels and permit blood to flow again, and whilst dialysis can do the job of diseased kidneys, transplants can replace them all together. Medical innovation is constant, but despite what our modern hospitals offer, life, living and age do have their natural limits, for now. There is always something on the horizon though, promising increased life span, if not increased health span. There was no autopsy carried out on the body of Queen Victoria. If there had been, the doctor might have seen heart disease or cerebral pathology, or discovered incidental disease processes in other organs, not directly contributing to death, as they tend to appear in octogenarians.

Victoria knew that her days were numbered and so called her secretary to discuss the arrangements for her funeral and her burial. 'I should like to live a little longer,' she said, 'as I have a few things to settle.' There was not much discussion; she simply dictated and he wrote. Twelve pages later there were detailed plans including a list of the things Victoria wished to be buried with. She was the queen of sentimentality after all. Her coffin was to be filled with items including a plaster cast of her beloved Albert's hand, made just after his death. There was her wedding ring too, but that was not the only ring she took with her. It was kept secret from the family, or they would not have allowed it, but Victoria also went to her grave with a ring given to her by John Brown, her Highland servant and, many believe, her lover. She also took a cutting from John Brown's hair and a photo of her

Highlander. It is not hard to imagine her son Bertie's fury had he known, but it was kept from him in an agreement between the Queen and her physician, Sir James Reid.

There were cut flowers laid around her body which hid the items below, and specifically some heather, a tribute to the beautiful landscape of the Highlands and her estate at Balmoral. She and Albert had built their castle, and it was where she felt relaxed and had the fortune to meet John Brown.

She asked to be buried in white. It is hard to conjure an image of the queen we think of as being in black mourning attire for decades, being dressed for ever after in white. Her dress was topped off with the lace veil that she wore on her wedding day. She also requested that in mourning her, the public should wear white. She was to be buried with an embroidered cape that had belonged to Albert, a gift from their daughter Alice who had died of diphtheria in 1878.

It was not the norm for our kings and queens to be buried with all their jewellery as it was in ancient cultures. Victoria requested that as much as could fit on her body should go to the grave with her. So, bracelets, necklaces and rings were laid upon her body. It was not just any old costume jewellery. They were items that held much significance for her, they were sentimental pieces.

In a full military affair, sailors and soldiers lined the streets and cavalry led the parade of uniformed mourners. Drummers and brass musicians joined kilted Highlanders, flanked by mourning soldiers with their firearms pointing to the ground, in turn giving way to parades of civilians, moustachioed and top-hatted. Even a dog joined the parade of mourners, captured for ever on film.

Victoria was the first monarch to be photographed and filmed on her final journey.

When Prince Albert died so many years before, an effigy was made for his resting place at a new mausoleum at Frogmore Estate, just down the road from Windsor. Victoria too had one made so that when she died they would rest together, but it had not been needed for so long that it was shoved in a storeroom somewhere and could not be found upon her death. Decades later it eventually came to light, was dusted off and added to the top of her plot.

Victoria's eldest son Bertie was waiting patiently for the crown, but he would have to wait a little longer for his coronation and for Edwardians to take centre stage.

Edward VII

Died 1910

Queen Victoria's eldest son and heir, who was named Albert, was deep in planning for his coronation to become Edward VII when he started to feel a niggle in his abdomen. Over the next few days, he felt sicker and sweat gathered on his forehead. This was not a good time to get sick. At fifty-nine years old, he had waited long enough for his coronation. A mass appeared in the lower right quadrant of his abdomen. He was not concerned enough to stop the plans and attended a banquet. The next day, enough was enough, and he was confined to bed. Eventually his doctors had to tell him that if he did not postpone his coronation and have an operation for appendicitis, then there was not going to be a coronation at all – he may as well plan his funeral. The King relented. Luckily for him, or perhaps because he was about to be crowned king, he was looked after by the foremost expert, Dr Frederick Treves, who had seen many an angry appendix. Treves cut open the King, lanced the abscess and washed out the infection. He sewed him back up and the King was smoking cigars in his bed the following day, according to the press. Edward lived and made it to his coronation after all.

It was not the first time that Bertie's life was threatened. Thirty years before, he had a brush with typhoid, the disease that likely killed his father. Queen Victoria must have hated 14 December. It was on this date in 1861 that her beloved Albert died of typhoid. Ten years to the day later, a young Bertie, her oldest son and heir, lay gravely ill of the same disease. On 14 December 1878 it was Princess Alice's turn. Having nursed her family members who had been struck down with diphtheria, Alice died of the disease herself.

Bertie was a petulant child and, his parents thought, lazy too. Always compared to his bright and articulate older sister Vicky, Bertie just shrugged it off, for he was the Prince of Wales. The young heir to the throne was more of a party animal than either of his parents, and so his popularity grew as he did. In his late teens he was sent to Canada with the Grenadier Guards to make a man of him. Well, it did do that, but not in the way Prince Albert intended. Bertie brought back a girl he had met, and gossip soon spread. She was not the last mistress in Bertie's bed though.

He was fifty-nine years old when he became king, the longest wait of any heir apparent until Prince Charles took that record to new heights. Despite all the worry and uncertainty that followed him around in his youth, he is remembered as an effective king. He reformed military roles and negotiated well in Europe. He spoke French and German and was related to most of the heads of state. At home though, there were issues.

Not taking any notice of his tobacco-hating distant relation James I, Edward VII was a heavy smoker. To get through twelve cigars and twenty cigarettes in one day was quite normal for him. Consequently, he was another king to not reach a decade on the throne. In April 1910 Edward became unwell. In May he suffered from a series of heart attacks until one killed him.

If Queen Victoria did die of a stroke then she succumbed to the current second most common cause of death, according to the World Health Organisation. Her son Bertie died of the current leading cause, ischaemic heart disease.

The associations between smoking and heart disease are strong. For Edward, the atherosclerosis did not just develop overnight on his trip to France, where he first collapsed in April of 1910. It started a lot earlier than that and developed with each puff on a cigarette. There were probably other factors too – diet, alcohol and genetics can all lead to a build-up of atherosclerotic plaques within blood vessels (hardening of the arteries). The rupture of plaques allows for more clot to be laid down around it until the artery becomes occluded and blood struggles to flow. It is not the huge vessels that take blood around the body to and from the heart that are affected, it is the coronary arteries themselves, the ones that supply the heart muscle with their oxygen. The heart muscle that had not stopped beating inside Bertie's chest for sixty-nine years was now being starved of oxygen. Edward's eyesight also failed as the oxygen could no longer be pumped to his brain to maintain vision.

Men over fifty were most likely to be the ones to drop down dead of heart disease or suffer angina on their way to doing so.

It was common to see a progression from the state of angina to unstoppable pain and collapse. Less than twenty years before King Edward VII's heart was being strangled, William Osler recognised that it was not the weak who died in this way, but strong men who lived life 'full speed ahead'. The middle-aged executive types who rush about and drop down dead.

Chronic lifestyle-related deaths are often preceded by high blood pressure, obesity, diabetes, obstructive lung disease and more. With each relapse into an unwell state, a decline happens, and though sufferers often rally, they are left worse off than the time before. There is usually a stepwise decline until the final illness. Edward VII's death is characteristic of a lot of our deaths today, from the diseases of the modern world related to diet and sedentary lives lived away from the sun and nature, with terrible sleep, and using alcohol, caffeine and other drugs as short-term fixes to long-term problems.

Edward lay in state at Westminster Hall with Gentlemen at Arms and Yeoman of the Guard watching over him along with officers of the Household Cavalry and Brigade of Guards. Millions of people watched the procession as his body was taken by gun carriage to Windsor. The sovereigns of Europe gathered round. Edward had been uncle to most of them.

George V

Died 1936

'*The King's life is moving peacefully towards its close.*'
Attributed to Bertrand Dawson,
1st Viscount Dawson of Penn

In 1865 George Frederick Ernest Albert, the son of Edward VII and Alexandra of Denmark, was born into the House of Hanover. As war raged against their German cousins in 1917, the family distanced themselves from this branch of relations with a change from the family name of Saxe-Coburg and Gotha to Windsor.

Young George and his brother were described by their grandmother Queen Victoria as ill-bred and ill-trained. They would run rings around everyone whilst their father rebelled against his own disciplined and stringent upbringing. This time, sending the young prince away to the Navy did result in the intended consequences. Unlike his father Edward, George learned the discipline and fortitude that would prove important in the years to come.

Once again it was the second son who became the king. His older brother Prince Albert Victor died at the age of twenty-eight of influenza during a pandemic in 1891. The tiny flu virus buried itself in the prince's respiratory epithelium. He would have had that familiar feeling, starting with a sore throat, followed by headache, aching joints and a rising temperature. He would have been sneezing and coughing and felt muddle-headed. Where it replicated and multiplied in the warm and damp, the flu virus found the perfect environment in the prince's lungs. The immune response recruited to the area would have created inflammation which impeded airflow and gas exchange. When an infected person coughs or sneezes, the virus is aerosolised and it moves on to the next warm damp throat. Prince Albert Victor died. There was much love for the heir despite his questionable morals and embarrassing antics. There was great shock and sadness when he passed away, apart from amongst those who have accused him of being Jack the Ripper. Prince Eddy, as he was known, had been engaged to be married to Mary of Teck. After his death she went on to marry his brother George.

Together George and Mary were king and queen during the First World War and whilst some scoffed at the royals for being plain and living too much on a par with their subjects, many more warmed to them, finding them likable. The King was robust enough to visit the Western Front but while he was there he had a fall from his horse, cracking his pelvis. He survived but his health faced a far worse scare a decade later in 1928 when he became severely ill and came close to dying. His physician, Lord Dawson, found an empyema (an abscess in his lung) and drained the pus from it, but the King developed sepsis. Enduring once again, he returned to London to crowds lining the streets, grateful for the King's survival. From then on, nothing was the same. A lifetime of heavy smoking took its toll, and his lungs were damaged. He developed chronic obstructive lung disease and suffered frequently from chest infections.

With chronic obstructive pulmonary disease, George endured a progressive breathlessness and an annoying persistent cough. With each strained cough a foul glob of mucus would come up from his airways into his mouth. The airways were narrowed with the inflammation, making it hard to breath out fully, trapping air in his chest. His air sacs were destroyed by the progressive disease, making each of his breaths less and less efficient.

Deaths from such chronic lung disease, after years of the destruction brought on by smoking, are rarely sudden. Sufferers will have acute attacks, often infective exacerbations of their illness. Each time they recover it's not to previous capacity. With each setback there is a step down in function until an insurmountable final episode is reached.

The death of King George V, whilst on the face of it yet another death brought on by modern lifestyle choices, had an extra helping hand along the way. Some have even gone so far as to suggest murder, that George was intentionally poisoned – a regicide in the twentieth century.

In January 1936 King George was too weak to attend a meeting of the Privy Council, complaining of a cold and taking to his bed. On 17 January Queen Mary called for Lord Dawson to come and attend to her failing husband. There was no lung abscess that could be drained this time. The King was gravely ill.

As George lay dying of respiratory and heart disease, the Archbishop of Canterbury, Cosmo Gordon Laing, prayed by his unconscious sovereign. Once the cleric was gone, Lord Dawson made a decision. He issued the statement that 'The King's life is moving peacefully towards its close.' He felt that the timing of the King's death was going to be critical. He was thinking only of the headlines. If the news was to go out first in the broadsheets, his preferred newspapers, then he would need to act. If the King died during the daytime, after the publication of the broadsheets, then the news would first be seen in the tabloids. He did not want such an undignified announcement. The King needed to die at night so that the news would reach the public in the respectable morning broadsheets. After asking his wife to inform *The Times* of the forthcoming news, he loaded his syringe with morphine and cocaine, and he helped the King pass away. 'I therefore decided to determine the end and injected morphia gr.3/4 and shortly afterwards cocaine gr.1 into the distended jugular vein.' The jugular vein in the King's neck was bulging as his heart struggled to maintain his life. The needle punctured the skin of his neck, and the drugs were pushed into his blood.

Though the Archbishop had commented that George did not appear to be in pain, his medications may have helped give that impression. In the King's peripheral nervous system, from the nerves around his lungs, sensors were recognising the damage and sending pain stimuli to the neurons in the spinal cord. The signals would have been transmitted up the spinal cord to the thalamus in the brain and on to the somatosensory cortex where George perceived the pain. Were he without analgesia, with each breath the King would have felt the pains in his chest and through to his back worsen. He would have moved about in the bed, trying to relieve the pain, to no avail. His doctor prescribed pain relief of opioids.

Opioids, injected into his blood via a vein, would act on receptors of the central nervous system's neuron cell membranes to provide analgesia and euphoria. They prevent release of neuro-transmitters from the synapse between the cells, thus putting a halt to forward momentum of any signals along the nerves. Opioids bring relief but they bring problems too. Escalation of the dose of morphine is limited by the side effects, primarily the effect it has on the breathing. Morphine depresses the respiratory system. On being injected with the morphine, George would have taken fewer and fewer breaths until he was no longer taking enough to get oxygen in, get carbon dioxide out and sustain life. There is an antidote to morphine overdose, known as Naloxone, it is carried by paramedics and emergency medical staff to help those who have overdosed on morphine substances like diamor-phine or heroin. It counters the depression of breathing, keeping air moving whilst other help can be given. It was just such a depression of breathing that ended George V's life. Dawson wrote that his decision was based on the timing of the news, a very twentieth-century decision. Though the news of the event was clearly on Dawson's mind, there was slightly more to it than that.

Morphine is commonly used at the end of life to relieve the pain and suffering in the last days. The dose of morphine required is patient dependent, it should be titrated for an effective dose, but too much would mean a premature death. Expediting a death is dependent on the patient's response. The doctor knew what he was doing. He had already instructed his wife to call his favoured newspaper even though it is impossible to predict the exact moment of someone's death, even for an experienced doctor.

Dawson was vocal about euthanasia. He believed doctor-delivered euthanasia in end-of-life situations was going to become the norm and he advocated for it. He believed that doctors should have the right to stop the pain and misery of anyone's last days of terminal illness. He also argued in the House of Lords that this should not be legalised, rather that it should be kept to the discretion of the doctors involved. Dawson had served at the Western Front during the First World War and was well respected. He was president of the Royal College of Physicians as well as president of the British Medical Association. Though he believed that the general stance on euthanasia would change, when his diaries came to light in the 1980s, long after his own death, many condemned his actions as nothing more than arrogant murder. Whilst the argument continues, euthanasia remains illegal.

Euthanasia has always been highly controversial, with far-reaching consequences for medical ethics, particularly regarding non-maleficence and the obligation to first doing no harm. Perhaps euthanasia should have been discussed with the physicians of Charles II, Queen Anne or even George III, who all saw their patients suffer terribly. The intention of those physicians though was likely to try everything to save the king or queen. The scenario in 1936 was different, as Dawson believed he was doing the right thing by relieving the King's pain by killing him. Technically, Dawson's act was regicide, whatever one might feel about it. Eighty-odd years later, the argument rages on. Was the doctor acting to relieve his King's pain or was he merely thinking of the newspaper timings? How much of a say did George V get regarding the end of his own life? Ironically, the King notoriously loathed the newspapers, calling them 'those filthy rags', and his final moments were predicated on which of them would convey the news of his end.

It was not discovered that Lord Dawson had used morphine and cocaine to end the King's life until the physician himself was dead. His diaries were found long after he had passed away and so the doctor couldn't defend his actions. Francis Watson published his biography, *Lord Dawson of Penn*, in the 1950s but made no mention of the incident. He had revealed some years later that he regretted not mentioning it, but that he had respected Dawson's widow's request to omit it.

Lord Dawson did not stop with the King. It is likely that he euthanised the King's sister, who became ill whilst on a trip to London in 1938. The doctor died in 1945 but he may have heard of the clerihew that was being muttered about him.

> *Lord Dawson of Penn*
> *Killed many men.*
> *That's why we sing*
> *'God Save the King'*

In his last moments, George V was said to have enquired after his empire. Famous last words are always dubious. It was also said that after it was put to him that he might travel to Bognor

Regis to recuperate, he replied with the wonderful retort, 'Bugger Bognor.' It was more likely that it was to Catherine Black, his nurse, that George addressed his last words. Catherine Black had been appointed as private nurse to George V after his episode of illness in 1928. She had served as a nurse during the First World War and had been a friend of Edith Cavell. Known as Blackie to members of the royal household, she was given her own rooms at Buckingham Palace. As she injected the King with a sedative, Dawson wrote in his diary that George had mumbled his last words: 'God damn you.' Nurse Black never made any comment on the events of the King's last night. We'll never know what she saw or heard.

Nearly one million mourners turned out to file past the King's body as he lay in state at Westminster Hall in 1936. He was laid to rest first in the royal vault but was later moved to within St George's Chapel, Windsor. George was succeeded by his son and heir Edward VIII but he did not hold out much hope. He had said of Edward that 'After I am dead, the boy will ruin himself in twelve months.'

Edward VIII

Died 1972

> *'I have found it impossible to carry on the heavy burden of responsibility and to discharge the duties of a king.'*
> Edward VIII's abdication speech

Nine hundred years after William earned the nickname The Conqueror, the royals were still calling each other names. Prince Albert, the first son of George V and Mary of Teck, was affectionately known as David.

Unlike his own father Edward VII, George V was a rather strict disciplinarian and treated his own children as Queen Victoria might have. The result was a next generation of anxious and fidgety youngsters.

The eldest son of George V and heir apparent came of age in an era of a well-established press. He was a hugely followed and much photographed young man and the public saw a party-loving socialite. He was a popular party animal who sent gossip columns into a spin. He was seen as a symbol of the societal changes that occurred after the Great War, but very much not as a good candidate to be king.

Biographies of Edward VIII are not particularly forgiving or even kind. There is a theory that a mumps infection at puberty left Edward underdeveloped and lacking in maturity into adulthood. It was said that the party-boy never grew up and lacked the backbone required for the responsibility of being king. There could be truth in it, but opinions about the King could also reflect mid-twentieth-century and contemporary attitudes towards masculinity. It was perhaps easiest to blame a medical mechanism for why he was not man enough to be king. It was a familiar accusation that had been levelled at his father George V as a young man too. But while the throne settled the old king at the start of the century, it did the opposite with Edward twenty-six years later. Within a year or two of his abdication, biographies were making inevitable comparisons with his grandfather.

On 20 January 1936, David learned that his father was dead and that he had become King Edward VIII. Complications were brewing. He already had plans to elope with his love, the charismatic Wallis Simpson. These plans had to be put on the back burner. She was divorced once from an abusive alcoholic and was married again, this time to a businessman named Simpson. The scandal of her affair with the King was kept quiet by the British press for a while, but the rest of the world started to comment and she had to file for divorce. For Edward this was the chance to marry his love, but the Government had other ideas. They had a veto over who would become his wife and they would not accept a twice-divorced American as queen consort. Marry her or else be king, they warned. Edward chose Simpson. The British people were not amused. There followed a constitutional, social and political crisis. The King left; he became the Duke of Windsor. He married Wallis and lived a life of luxury with not much to do except for encouraging Hitler and settling in France after the war.

In 1964 our old friend the American surgeon Michael DeBakey successfully operated on Edward's abdominal aortic aneurysm. We might have been discussing a death scene not unlike George II in 1760 otherwise.

In 1971, Edward brought a cigarette up to his mouth and took a long, hard drag. Was his throat feeling a little sore? He had noticed a hoarseness this morning. Thirty-six years after he abdicated the throne to his younger brother, the Duke of Windsor was ravaged by the wasting effects of cancer of the throat. Edward's hedonistic days of wealthy leisure had caught up with his body. At first he would have had difficulty in swallowing and he may have noticed a change in his voice. These cancers tend to grow quickly and as with many cancer sufferers, the body wastes and becomes cachectic. He was treated with cobalt therapy, the medical use of gamma rays from radioisotope Cobalt-60, to treat the cancerous tissues.

The very word cancer strikes fear into most of us, so much that we use euphemisms to avoid the C word. Very little is known of the history of cancers. In the previous centuries it was communicable diseases and the threat of infection that caused such dread: smallpox, sweating sickness and plague. By the later part of the twentieth century, when infectious diseases were seen less and life expectancy increased, we started to see more cancers responsible for deaths. When cancers were seen in centuries past they were thought to be the result of imbalance of the humour black bile. In Edward's throat there was no stagnation of black bile, but living tissues, tickled and rubbed by noxious substances, such as tar in cigarettes, that started to behave abnormally.

Cells die all the time to be replenished and replaced, but in Edward's cancerous tissue the ability of the cells to develop into what they should be was disrupted. There are six characteristics that all cancer cells have. They divide without limits and grow without direction or influence from the outside such as hormones. They engage in angiogenesis, the development of new blood vessels, to bring themselves blood supply. They ignore STOP signals. They do not respond to apoptosis or programmed cell death. They metastasise, spreading to other parts of the body.

Eighty per cent of cancers arise in the epithelial cells that make up the linings of organs and the skin. The older you are, the more likely that you will develop cancer and be exposed to carcinogens. Environmental factors that cause cells to transform into cancerous growths were first described by Percivall Pott, a Victorian physician. He noticed that young boys who were sent naked up chimneys to sweep out the soot were susceptible to scrotal cancers, and he connected it to their brushing against the soot collected on the chimney walls. The tars in the soot that rubbed against the boys' skin caused the reaction of the cells to form cancers. The lining of Edward's throat in response to years of inhaled cigarette smoke and alcohol consumption did the same thing. Throat cancers can also be caused by an infective agent. The human papillomavirus that causes cervical cancers can also cause cancers of the throat in the same manner. Youngsters are now routinely vaccinated against this virus.

In 1972 as the Duke of Windsor was dying, he was visited by the Queen. Her own father, who had been given the throne when Edward ran from it, had died twenty years before. In this awkward moment between a present and a former monarch, Edward was so weakened that he could hardly stand. King for less than one year, the shortest-reigning of all the monarchs (if we are not counting Lady Jane Grey), he died in 1972 at seventy-seven years old.

Edward's body was brought back to England from France; by now it was far easier than it had been for his twelfth-century predecessors. His body lay in state at St George's Chapel, Windsor before being buried. Edward lies under a simple stone slab at the royal burial ground at Frogmore. In 1986 the Duchess whom he gave up his throne for, Wallis Simpson, was buried alongside him after her own decline into dementia.

After Edward's abdication, once again the succession had turned to a younger brother. Bertie became George VI, and he was just what was needed as war with Europe sat ominously on the horizon.

George VI

Died 1952

I feel burnt out.

After all our stories of trauma, regicide, accidents, intrigue, disease and drama, the last monarch died peacefully in his own bed in 1952.

Despite primogeniture, the passing of the crown from monarch to first-born son, young Bertie was yet another second son who became king. In 1936 his brother Edward VIII abdicated and left him in the lurch. Bertie was forty years old.

As his wayward brother was set to become king, Bertie joined the Royal Navy but was not an exceptional student and came bottom of his graduating class. He suffered a bout of pneumonia whilst at the naval college at Osborne. Later, during the First World War, he joined the flyers and was certified a pilot. Still he had medical problems. He underwent surgery for appendicitis at the start of the war and had to spend time away recuperating. He fought at the Battle of Jutland in 1916 but went under the knife again in 1917, this time for a duodenal ulcer. Known to many from the movie *The King's Speech*, he developed a marked stammer in childhood. He was prone to tears and temper tantrums – that disciplined upbringing unhelpfully rearing its head again.

By the time the Second World War had begun, Bertie had become King George VI. Compared to his brother's short-lived neglect of business, he steadied the ship and the way he conducted himself during the war was commendable. He and his wife Queen Elizabeth stayed at Buckingham Palace during German bombing raids but, unlike so many, came out of it unharmed. The King and Queen boosted national morale during the war, visiting, meeting and greeting.

The Second World War had taken a huge toll on the King and his health. 'I feel burnt out,' he confessed. Like his father and brother, George was a heavy smoker and suffered the consequences. He was diagnosed with Buerger's disease, another illness that has a strong association with smoking. Buerger's, officially *thromboangiitis obliterans*, affects the arteries with progressive thrombosis causing inflammation. George would have felt pain in his feet, tracking up his legs. He would have noticed an alarming change in the colour of his limbs, perhaps a pallor at first, later the dusky blue of cyanosis. His hands and feet would have been incredibly sensitive to the cold of a British winter. Buerger's can lead to amputations if the ulcerations progress to gangrene. George did not get that far, but he had other problems. For a start his physicians would have known that peripheral vascular disease is usually accompanied by similar pathology more centrally, in the vessels of his heart or in his brain. They would be worried about coronary heart disease and stroke.

As well as Buerger's causing claudication (pain in the calves, thighs or buttocks), the King was diagnosed with atherosclerosis. There was an accumulation of inflammatory material on the inner layers of his coronary artery walls. Macrophages (immune cells), lipids, calcium and fibrous connective tissue caused a sticky build-up. In some cases the build-up can block off the arteries' lumen and increase the chances of plaque rupture and more thrombosis development.

On top of heart disease, George was also diagnosed with cancer of the lung. In September 1951 the King went under the knife again. This time he was told rather euphemistically that it was for 'structural abnormalities'. A left total pneumonectomy meant that they took out his left lung. The doctors kept the diagnosis quiet from the public, and from the King himself. He was well enough to wave off Princess Elizabeth and her husband Philip on their tour of Africa, but not long after the King died unexpectedly in his sleep. His valet found him dead when he arrived at his room early in the morning.

With the previous diagnoses of peripheral vascular disease and atherosclerosis, George VI's death was put down to coronary heart disease. Cardiovascular pathologists have had other ideas as recently as 2021. With George still coughing up blood after the pneumonectomy, it is likely that the disease was in his right lung also. Pulmonary embolism or intrathoracic haemorrhage are both complications of bronchogenic carcinoma that could have killed the King unexpectedly in the night. Whilst coronary thrombosis could have caused his sudden death, it is now thought that the lung cancer persisted after his operation and so it is that that killed him.

The official line for a while now, upon the death of a royal family member, has been that 'they died peacefully in their sleep'. That is what was said of George VI. Gone are the days of battlefield monarchs facing gangrenous crossbow wounds, red-hot pokers in undesired areas and the ever-present threat of poison. Now, like the rest of their subjects, kings and queens are more likely to succumb to the chronic lifestyle-related conditions that kill most of their subjects in the twenty-first century. For George VI, the primary culprit was his heavy smoking.

His wife Elizabeth became Queen Elizabeth, the Queen Mother, and outlived her husband by half a century. When she died in 2002 at the age of 101, she was buried with her husband and their second daughter Princess Margaret at St George's Chapel at Windsor. The Queen Mother asked that the wreath from her coffin be taken and laid at the Tomb of the Unknown Warrior at Westminster Abbey.

The King and his wife Elizabeth had two daughters. When news spread that George VI had died, London came to a momentary standstill as people got out of their cars, and shut their shops and offices to show their respect for their wartime king. In Kenya his daughter Elizabeth was informed that she was now the Queen.

Queen Elizabeth II has been the longest-reigning of all the British monarchs, celebrating 70 years on the throne in 2022.

Long live the Queen.

Elizabeth II

Died 2022

*'I declare before you all that my whole life whether it be long
or short shall be devoted to your service'*

Elizabeth II, 1947

On Tuesday, 6 September 2022, the rain was falling heavily on the Queen's Balmoral estate in Scotland. All eyes were looking through the storms towards her Scottish residence as the ninety-six-year-old monarch's mobility problems prevented her from travelling to London. Instead of the Queen making the journey south, two Prime Ministers, the outgoing Boris Johnson and the incoming Liz Truss, came north to Balmoral to see her. The news reporters and press photographers followed and a photograph of the Queen was released. She looked more frail than anyone had lately seen her, yet she smiled as warmly as she always had during her reign of longer than seventy years. Only two days later the world's media camera crews were back at Balmoral Castle; this time they were wearing black.

On the morning of 8 September, news started to spread that the Queen was unwell. The doctors had concerns, the reports said, and the Queen was under medical care. Britain's longest-reigning monarch was ailing. A few months earlier, in the summer sunshine, the Queen, the country and the commonwealth had celebrated her Platinum Jubilee, marking seventy years on the throne. Now in the rains of autumn, the Queen was dying.

Elizabeth was ten years old in 1936 when her father became king. Until then she was merely the daughter of the Duke of York. Life had been a carefree existence for the young Elizabeth and her sister Margaret, with any idea of her one day becoming Queen a distant thought, as her healthy uncle became Edward VIII. He would likely marry and have children and they would inherit the crown. However, within a year of George V's death, and rather suddenly, her uncle abdicated. Elizabeth became heir presumptive. That meant that she was next in the line of succession, unless her father had a son, in which case, she would be pushed down the list in her hypothetical brother's favour, despite being the first born. But there was no brother and so, in 1952 when her father George VI died and she was just twenty-five years old, she became Queen Elizabeth II.

Elizabeth had met the dashing and rather charming Philip of Greece when she was thirteen. They shared a great-great-grand-mother in Queen Victoria, and Philip's father had been King of Greece and Denmark, though following the 1922 Greek revolution the family were exiled from Greece when Philip was only eighteen months old. The prince's mother, Princess Alice of Battenberg, was later institutionalised after suffering a breakdown.

By marrying Elizabeth, Prince Philip steadied the family ship. The couple had married in 1947 and, when she became Queen, he supported her for the rest of his life, becoming the longest serving of all royal consorts.

Prince Philip, the Duke of Edinburgh, died in 2021, of old age. He was ninety-nine years old. This triggered Operation Forth Bridge, named as a hat tip to his dukedom city of Edinburgh. It was a comprehensive plan for what was to happen when he died, including who would be invited to the funeral service. It also stated that his coffin be carried on a specially converted Land Rover designed by the Prince himself. The funeral took place during the Covid pandemic restrictions. Even though the Queen had been photographed so much throughout her life, the extraordinary image of her sitting alone, mourning her late husband, was instantly one of the most iconic photos of her ever taken.

Seventeen months later, the Queen's family would themselves be photographed mourning their loss of her. Her Majesty had many years ago agreed two protocols to be enacted when she died: Operation London Bridge and Operation Unicorn. The codewords to be used were 'London Bridge is down'. These codewords were designed to avoid any phone operators overhearing the news of a royal death before the palace made an official announcement. When George VI died the protocol was named Operation Hyde Park Corner; Operation Tay Bridge was used for the Queen Mother and the name of the plan to be enacted when King Charles III dies is Operation Menai Bridge, as he was for so long the Prince of Wales. Whilst there will always be a family member, however distant, to step up to the throne when a monarch dies, one can't help but wonder if they might run out of bridges.

Operation London Bridge included details of how the announcement of the Queen's death was to be made, which images should be displayed on television screens, which flowers be placed on the coffin, who would be standing vigil as she lay in state and where she would be interred.

Operation Unicorn was not quite as well known and would only come into effect should Elizabeth die in Scotland. A British monarch had not died in Scotland for almost five hundred years, since James V of Scotland was said to have collapsed of a broken heart in 1542 when he heard he had lost the Battle of Solway Moss to the English. Queen Victoria had bought Balmoral estate in 1852 and every year Elizabeth and her family escaped there, to enjoy the tranquility of the Highlands. There was always a chance that Operation Unicorn – so named because unicorns are the national animal of Scotland, honest – might be required. This operation detailed the logistics of moving the Queen's body to Edinburgh where there would be a Scottish memorial at St Giles Cathedral before she travelled on her final journey south of the border.

In this new century, this was no longer a time of waiting for the broadsheet newspapers as it had been for her grandfather's death. The Queen's coronation had been the first to be televised, and now her death was going to be announced on television too by the BBC. In the evening, reporter Huw Edwards, wearing a black tie, told the nation that Buckingham Palace had announced the death of Her Majesty the Queen. She died peacefully at

Balmoral, the palace said. There would be ten days of national mourning to follow. The news spread around the world in an instant. Blackened billboards throughout the UK set the somber tone for the ten days ahead.

At the gates of Balmoral, people came from all over Scotland to pay their respects, bring flowers, see the spectacle and be part of an historic occasion. The mood was solemn, and the only sounds were the hum of the international press, saying their pieces to camera, describing the scene. I took my eighty-four-year-old mother-in-law, so she could lay some flowers. She remembers the death of the previous monarch over seventy years before. There aren't many left that do.

The Queen's coffin was draped in a flag and driven first to Aberdeen, on to Edinburgh and then south to London. It was there for all to see in a big-windowed hearse, by those lining the streets or watching on the internet. However, not everyone believed the Queen was in the coffin. In an age of social media, nobody is afraid of shouting out their thoughts for fear of being beheaded. Some baselessly believe that the Queen was cremated at Balmoral Castle, the only evidence being her sister Margaret was cremated. Had this been written by a monk in an ancient chronicle, we might still be telling the legend today. Perhaps this story will become part of tomorrow's folklore. Whether empty or not, the coffin made the long journey to London, to rest for a while at Westminster Hall.

Then came the queue. One joined The Queue, which very quickly became an entity worthy of a capital letter, to walk past the Queen's coffin as she lay in state at Westminster Hall. There the mourners were met by the royal guard, members of the military and even at one point by the new king and the royal family. An estimated 250,000 people paid their respects. The Queue was ten miles long at one point and mourners could wait for as long as a day. The Queue became, for a short while, as talked about as the Queen, with books, screenplays, love stories and crime fiction already being written about it.

Once the last person in The Queue had moved out of the hall, arrangements for the funeral were set in motion. The Queen's funeral became the most watched television broadcast in history. In Britain it was declared a bank holiday. With everything shut, there was nothing else to do. Her oak coffin, lined with lead, reportedly weighed over 500 pounds and the world collectively held their breaths as the guardsmen moved it from plinth to gun carriage and back again. In a military procession from Buckingham Palace to Westminster Abbey and then on to Windsor, the Queen made her final journey. The Lord Chamberlain's wand of office, a wooden staff signifying his role, was broken over the coffin to signify the end of the Lord Chamberlain's service to Queen Elizabeth as sovereign. At the committal service at Windsor's St George's Chapel, the coffin was lowered into the vault below to the sound of a lone piper's lament. Prince Philip, who had been interred in a temporary vault during his funeral some months before, was buried by her side in their final resting place.

Elizabeth II's death certificate, which is in the public domain in Scotland and available to see in the National Records, tells a simple story. Cause of death 1A: Old Age. Her death was certified by Dr Douglas Glass, Apothecary to Her Majesty's Household. It sounds like a 250-year-old pharmacist signed the form, but this is an old honorary title given some years ago to the local GP for his service to the household at Balmoral. As a historian I would like to ask Dr Glass, who just happens to be my own GP, about writing the death certificate. As a doctor I understand confidentiality and I wouldn't put him in that awkward position. Unless I see him at our local pub, then I might buy him a dram and see.

When the death certificate was released three weeks after her death, letters were quickly scribbled to news editors, complaining that 'old age' was misleading. Reporters rushed to question the validity of such a claim. 'The officials are trying to pull the wool over our eyes,' they said, seeking a more specific cause of death. Despite the scratching of heads, in Scotland it is considered a perfectly reasonable thing to write on the death certificate of somebody who has died at ninety-six years of age.

Whatever actual physiological or pathological event is occurring, the phrase 'old age' as a cause of death is somehow easier to swallow. It feels like a calm, slow descent into sleep. It tells us nothing of the burden of pain that a diagnosis of cancer might. It tells us nothing of the burden of breathlessness that a diagnosis of COPD might. It tells us nothing of the burden to everyone that a diagnosis of dementia might. It feels peaceful. It almost seems like it is written to appease the reader. Yet something was underlying the cause of death. Why, I was asked, was it not written that she had a cardiac arrest? Cardiac arrest makes less sense than 'old age' as, ultimately, everyone dies with a cardiac arrest – all our hearts will stop when we die. 'Natural circumstances' is a difficult phrase too. After all, arsenic is natural. OK, historically that's a poor example considering how common poisoning accusations are when a monarch dies, but for once these are absent here.

'It was expected and we were quite aware of what was going to happen,' Dr Glass was quoted in Gyles Brandreth's *Elizabeth: An intimate portrait*. In the book, Brandreth claims that the real cause of death of Queen Elizabeth was a bone marrow cancer. His claim quickly spread and in some corners it was misquoted as bone cancer. They are two different entities, but both cancers none the less.

Bone marrow cancers cause abnormal growth of the cells within the marrow. Marrow is the spongy fatty tissue at the centre of some bones that produces the blood cells – red cells of oxygen carriage, white cells of the immune system – and platelets, involved in clotting. These cancers include the leukaemias and myeloma. They are categorised according to which cell or component is affected. A diagnosis of such a cancer would be identified through signs, symptoms and blood analysis. At ninety-six years old, treatment for such a disease is challenging. Some choose not to face those treatments but live out what time they have remaining without serious medical intervention.

Regardless of any unnamed associated pathology that caused the death, there are, at a cellular level, problems associated with old age. DNA can't replicate and produce new proteins for ever. At the end of each chromosome, there are structures called telomeres. They have to be there because of the way the mechanism of replication works. Every time a gene is replicated, a little of it has to be chopped off and is permanently lost. Telomeres are effectively built in redundancy, designed to be sacrificed to keep the integrity of the crucial information needed to make the protein. Eventually even the telomeres run out and genes become exhausted. They can't multiply any more, and so can't make new proteins that are still the same structure. With increasingly more faulty proteins, the cells and organs will no longer perform so efficiently. The familiar outwards signs of aging become more pronounced. Pounded by environmental factors, lifestyle, exercise, genetics, diet and vices, our cells and bodies are not designed to go on for ever.

Over the course of Elizabeth's life and reign there were so many notable events, so much change whilst she remained steadfast. The most striking change since the death of her father seventy years before was the growth of instant worldwide communication. Even with this technology and ability to spread information, similar speculations that had followed the deaths of British monarchs for the last 1,000 years were being voiced in 2022. Was she really dead? Or had she been dead for years? Was she in the coffin at all? What happened to her body? Did she take anything with her to the grave? Instead of clarifying everything, the internet allowed the rumours to spread quickly – it's almost, we might say, a rite of passage for our departing monarchs. What's clear, however, was the loudest message of all: this was a beloved monarch, a good queen. We'll remember that her death was kind and peaceful; the nation, and the world, will remember her with affection.

Elizabeth's legacy leaves a far less bitter taste or putrid smell than many monarchy deaths over the last 1,000 years. Without any succession drama, without any suspicions of poison and without any falling out with the church, the transition was a smooth one, calm and controlled, just like the Queen herself and her reign. Queen Elizabeth's son and heir, Charles, became King Charles III at the age of seventy-three.

Long live the King.

Selected Bibliography

Appleby, J. et al, 'Perimortem Trauma in King Richard III: a skeletal analysis, *The Lancet*, Vol. 385, No. 9964 (2015), pp.253–9

Brewer, C., *The Death of Kings: A Medical History of the Kings and Queens of England* (Abson Books, 2000)

Burch, D., *Digging up the Dead: Uncovering the Life and Times of an Extraordinary Surgeon* (Chatto & Windus, 2007)

Chibnall, M., *Anglo-Norman England 1066–1166* (Wiley-Blackwell, 1987)

Chibnall, M., *The World of Orderic Vitalis: Norman Monks and Norman Knights* (Boydell & Brewer, 1996)

Crawfurd, R., *The Last Days of Charles II* (Clarendon Press, 1909)

Douglas, D. C., *William the Conqueror: The Norman Impact Upon England* (University of California Press, 1964)

Engel, H., *Lord High Executioner: An Unashamed Look at Hangmen, Headsmen, and Their Kind* (Robson Books, 1997)

Emson, H. E., 'For the want of an heir: the obstetrical history of Queen Anne', *British Medical Journal*, Vol. 304, No. 6838 (1992), pp.136–6

Erickson, C., *Bloody Mary: The Life of Mary Tudor* (St Martin's Press, 2007)

Erickson, C., *Brief Lives of The English Monarchs: From William the Conqueror to Elizabeth II* (Constable, 2007)

Evans, M., *The Death of Kings: Royal Deaths in Medieval England* (Bloomsbury Academic, 2006)

Fitzharris, L., *The Butchering Art: Joseph Lister's Quest to Transform the Grisly World of Victorian Medicine* (Penguin, 2017)

Fraser, A., *King Charles II* (Weidenfeld & Nicholson, 2011)

Goodall, A. L., 'The Health of James the Sixth of Scotland and First of England', *Medical History* (1957), pp.17–27

Gillingham, J., 'The unromantic death of Richard I', *Speculum*, Vol. 54(1) (1979), pp.18–41

Glynn, I and J., *The Life and Death of Smallpox* (Profile, 2004)

Holmes, G. F., 'The Death of Young King Edward VI', *New England Journal of Medicine*, Vol. 345(1) (2001), pp.60–61

Holmes, F., The *Sickly Stuarts: The Medical Downfall of a Dynasty* (Sutton, 2003)

Horspool, D., *The English Rebel: One Thousand Years of Trouble-making from the Normans to the Nineties* (Viking, 2009)

Hutchinson, R., *The Last Days of Henry VIII: Conspiracy, Treason and Heresy at the Court of the Dying Tyrant* (Weidenfeld & Nicholson, 2011)

King, E., 'Stephen of Blois, Count of Mortain and Boulogne', *The English Historical Review*, Vol. 115, No. 461 (2000), pp.271–96

Selected Bibliography

Knappen, M. M., 'The Abdication of Edward VIII', *The Journal of Modern History*, Vol. 10 (2) (1938), pp.242–50

Keynes, M., 'The Aching Head and Increasing Blindness of Queen Mary I', *Journal of Medical Biography*, Vol, 8 (2) (2000), pp.102–109

Kean, S., *The Tale of the Duelling Neurosurgeons: The History of the Human Brain as Revealed by True Stories of Trauma, Madness, and Recovery* (Transworld, 2014)

Lacey, R., *Great Tales from English History: Cheddar Man to the Peasants' Revolt* (Little, Brown, 2003)

Lamont-Brown, R., *Royal Poxes and Potions: The Lives of Court Physicians, Surgeons & Apothacaries* (The History Press, 2001)

MacArthur, W. P., 'The Cause Of The Death Of William, Duke Of Gloucester, Son Of Queen Anne, In 1700', *British Medical Journal*, Vol. 1, No. 3507 (1928), pp.502–503

Medvei, V. C., 'The Illness and Death of Mary Tudor', *Journal of the Royal Society of Medicine*, Vol. 80 (1987)

Mortimer, I., 'The Death of Edward II in Berkeley Castle" *The English Historical Review*, Vol. 120, No. 489 (2005). Pp.1175–1214

Mortimer, I., *The Perfect King: The Life of Edward III, Father of the English Nation* (Vintage, 2018)

Nuland, S. B., *How We Die* (Vintage, 1997)

Nuland S. B., *How We Live* (Vintage, 1998)

Nicholas, J., 'Nova et Vetera – Some Royal Death-Beds', *British Medical Journal*, Vol. 1, No. 1557 (1910)

Parsons, J. C. and B. Wheeler (eds), *Medieval Mothering* (Taylor & Francis, 1996)

Paxman, J., *On Royalty* (Penguin, 2006)

Schama, S., *A History of Britain 1: 3000BC–AD1603 At the Edge of the World?* (BBC, 2000)

Shrewsbury, J. F. D., 'Henry VIII: A Medical Study', *Journal of the History of Medicine and Allied Sciences*, Vol, 7 (2) (1952), pp.141–85

Skidmore, C., *Bosworth: The Birth of the Tudors* (Weidenfeld & Nicholson, 2013)

Spencer, C., *Killers of the King: The Men Who Dared to Execute Charles I* (Bloomsbury, 2014)

Spencer, C., *The White Ship: Conquest, Anarchy and the Wrecking of Henry I's Dream* (Harper Collins, 2020)

Strachey, L., *Queen Victoria* (Penguin Classics, 2000)

Acknowledgements

The late Dr Sherwin B. Nuland wrote books that made me want to be a doctor. He did not know it, but I always hoped to follow his footsteps, in my own way. It has been enormous fun trying. Thank you to Mr G. Patrick Ashcroft of Aberdeen's Orthopaedic department, who provided infectious enthusiasm and encouragement to follow my own path.

I owe much to Emily Glenister, my agent at DHH Literary Agency, who believed in my storytelling and calmly guided me through the ins and outs of publishing a book. Creating anything during the Covid-19 lockdown months was not easy. Without a doubt that tricky path was made easier to navigate with the help, enthusiasm and experience of Philip Connor. Thank you to Lucy Hall, Emily Patience, Jill Cole and the rest of the team at Wildfire and Headline.

Krishna Vakharia, Yvonne Beresford, Georgina Forbes, Louise Allan, Inge Kreuser-Genis, Toyin Ajayi, Katrina Butcher, Nicole

Goh, Nicky Wilson, Claudia Camden-Smith, Rachel Hudson, Kathryn Yu, Rachel Wallis and Charis Manganis are all dedicated doctors, understanding mothers and fearless cheerleaders, as well as being my friends. They have listened to me talk about my projects day and night and have sent encouragement, coffee and even on occasion, champagne.

Ryan Clark, Melissa Ratliff, Basma Greef and the Cambs online writing group gave me gentle nudges over the phone whenever I needed them. One day I may be able to thank them in person.

Thank you to my wonderful and kind followers on TikTok, from all over the world, some of whom have been commenting and encouraging from my very first human body history video. I appreciate you all and am grateful.

To the Edges: Derek, Kathryn and Charlotte and June, thank you. I hope you are ready to do this again because I appear to have caught the writing bug whilst digging about in all the dead bodies.

If you enjoyed *Mortal Monarchs*, look out
for Dr Suzie Edge's upcoming book,
Vital Organs – A journey through history's
most famous limbs, organs, and appendages . . .

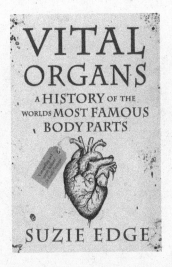

**From Napoleon's penis to Van Gogh's ear, from
Marie Antoinette's teeth to Marie Curie's bone
marrow, this book brings together the remarkable
stories of body parts that have made history.**

We have always used and abused bodies. We've torn them apart,
dug them up, experimented on them or taken bits home to
display as trophies. Body parts have been used for propaganda
in wars and pulled off in punishment. They've answered medical
mysteries, been turned into relics and even saved lives.

Now TikTok sensation and medical historian, Dr Suzie
Edge, brings us a history of the world's most famous body
parts told through its most notable limbs, organs, and
appendages, including how Queen Victoria's armpit led the
development of antiseptics; why Percy Shelley's heart refused
to burn; and the strange case of Hitler's right testicle.